GROUPS TO GO

Small Groups For Counselors On The Go

18 Ready-To-Use Small-Group Counseling Plans For Grades 3-5

Two Groups For Each Topic:

Academic Improvement
At-Risk Behaviors
Decision Making
Divorce
Grief And Loss
Respect
Self-Confidence
Social Skills
Test Taking

**Written By
Arden Martenz**

Illustrated By Brian Dumm

GROUPS TO GO: SMALL GROUPS FOR COUNSELORS ON THE GO

10-DIGIT ISBN: 1-57543-143-2   13-DIGIT ISBN: 978-1-57543-143-7

COPYRIGHT © 2006 MAR*CO PRODUCTS, INC.
  Published by mar*co products, inc.
  1443 Old York Road
  Warminster, PA 18974
  1-800-448-2197
  www.marcoproducts.com

PRINTED IN THE U.S.A.

TABLE OF CONTENTS

WELCOME TO
GROUPS TO GO

Small-group counseling is the backbone of elementary counseling. It is the principal service no one in the school but a counselor is trained to provide. I once attended a seminar at which the speaker said, "Problems that originate in groups need to be addressed and solved in groups." Most problems facing young children are rooted in one group or another—peer groups or family groups. Hence, the importance of small-group counseling is self-evident.

Time is always a factor during the school day. There is always more to do than time allows. So if students are going to be removed from their classrooms, the amount of time they miss has to be minimal. The sessions in *Groups To Go: Small Groups For Counselors On The Go* are designed to be completed in 30-40 minutes, so you will find very few paper and pencil tasks and more interactive activities. Small-group counseling is a child's opportunity for expression and reflection. At first glance, the sessions may seem to be short. But once you and the children are involved in discussion, the time will pass quickly and productively.

The selected groups in *Groups To Go* have been used with children. Most have been adapted from issues of *PIC* (*Practical Ideas For Counselors*), a counselor newsletter which was written by Mar*co staff and contributing counselors. Unless otherwise specified, the groups in this book were written and conducted in the school system by counselors who were members of Mar*co's staff. They have been written to be as user-friendly as possible and include the techniques that proved most successful. However, each school is different. So is every child. Although each session includes step-by-step directions, you may find that you need to make adaptations to fit your particular situation. If necessary, adjust the sessions to give your students the best experience possible.

Some counselors like to present *Group Rules* at the beginning of a small-group counseling experience. Although these rules have not been included in the first sessions of the groups, counselors should feel free to add them to their lesson. You'll find an example of *Group Rules* in the *Grief And Loss* section on page 117.

Although *Groups To Go* has been created to make your small-group counseling program easy to initiate and continue, it must be remembered that:

GROUPS TO GO: SMALL GROUPS FOR COUNSELORS ON THE GO © 2006 MAR*CO PRODUCTS, INC. 1-800-448-2197

Nobody ever said group counseling was easy ...

Group counseling can be rewarding or frustrating for counselors. If the group members change their behavior, counselors feel a tremendous sense of satisfaction and pride. But when one member behaves in a way that stops the group from functioning, the group itself has no cohesion, or the leader just can't get control, being the leader becomes an experience many counselors do not want to repeat. To prevent this from happening, here are 10 tips on what to do when problems arise.

What can you do when one group member constantly disrupts the group?

Mary will not stop interrupting when another group member is talking. She is so determined to talk about her concerns that her talking dominates each group session.

Group counseling may not be the best way to work with this type of student. Carefully examine Mary's problem and her needs and ask yourself if her needs are so great that it is unreasonable to expect her to share counseling time with other students. If the answer to the question is "yes," it is most probable that Mary would benefit more from individual counseling. For this type of student, it is sometimes better to learn to relate to one person before attempting to relate to several people. Through individual counseling, the counselor can help Mary with her problem while helping her learn to function in a group. As progress is made, the counselor can have Mary spend part of her time with the group and part of her time in individual sessions, making sure that Mary is fully aware that the final goal is for her to be a functioning member of a group.

If, after examining the problem carefully, the counselor feels Mary would benefit from group counseling, group consequences must be set up for students who interrupt. An example of an appropriate consequence is that any interrupter would not be allowed to speak for the rest of the session. The consequence could be set up so that the interrupting student not only did not speak, but sat apart from the group and observed for the rest of the session. A counselor who uses this technique should ask the interrupting student to remain for a few minutes after the group has left so the two of them can discuss why the student was not part of the group and what the student must do to remain part of the group during subsequent sessions.

What can you do when one group member is always "picked on"?

According to the group, Mike is always doing something wrong. If he says something, the others criticize him. If he does something in class, the group reports it at the counseling session. No matter what happens in the group, it seems Mike is always to blame.

One group member will occasionally be singled out as a "troublemaker." In most cases, this is an unpopular student. Counselors can approach the problem in two ways.

First, determine whether the blame is justified. If it is, the counselor may conduct some group sessions that key in on individual students' problems rather than on a group problem. Place a chair so it faces the group members. Then tell the group that for the next few sessions, their task will be to help group members change their behavior. They can do this by being honest and telling the student sitting in the chair what they think he/she should change. The student sitting in the chair may not respond in any way while group members are talking. Begin by selecting any group member, except the one who is always blamed, to sit in the chair. Explain that each student will tell the person in the chair something he/she believes would help him/her be better liked. Then have each student make a statement to the student sitting in the chair. When each group member has had a turn, ask the student sitting in the chair to select one of the ideas expressed and make that change before the next session. Continue the exercise, using other group members and including the student who is always blamed. At the next session, have the group members report on how they performed their tasks. The counselor should encourage all the students to continue positive behavior with students for whom it would be helpful, or suggest making changes other than those mentioned previously.

If the counselor decides the blaming is not justified, the group rule that no one may "put down" another student should be enforced and consequences set up for those who break the rule. If the situation is critical, the counselor may decide to hold a session without the "picked-on" student to discuss what is going on and what can stop this group behavior.

What can you do when a group member doesn't participate?

David never has anything to contribute to group discussion. He sits quietly and apparently listens to what others say, but never volunteers. When asked his opinion, he says, "I don't know."

Shy students, students who have difficulty expressing thoughts or students who are insecure in groups often sit quietly and let others do all the talking. This can be frustrating because the counselor feels unable to reach these group members.

One way to involve this type of student is to vary the group activity. It is the counselor's responsibility to find ways to involve each group member, and if oral discussions do not meet everyone's needs, a different approach should be taken. Create an art activity that will fit into the group's purpose and have the students participate in it. When everyone has finished, have all the students share their drawings. This will give the non-verbal student like David something concrete to talk about. If he still has difficulty expressing himself, the counselor should sit near him and help him begin the task. If he still cannot participate, the counselor should evaluate whether group counseling is the best way to work with this student. A few individual counseling sessions may help the student feel more secure. Then he can return to the group.

GROUPS TO GO: SMALL GROUPS FOR COUNSELORS ON THE GO © 2006 MAR✶CO PRODUCTS, INC. 1-800-448-2197

What can you do if a group member breaks confidentiality?

Clarissa knew one of the rules of the group was that she could discuss anything she talked about, but nothing other group members talked about. After a discussion about family life, Clarissa went back to the classroom and told her best friend about the troubles another group member was having in his home.

In certain groups, the issue of confidentiality must be stressed as essential. To be certain that students understand, it may be necessary to remind them how vital this issue is before each session begins and again at the end of each session. Depending upon the age of the students, it also may be necessary to give examples of what can happen when a group member breaks confidentiality. Group members must realize that violating confidentiality can embarrass or hurt fellow group members and make them distrustful. Because of the importance of confidentiality, the leader should set up, at the beginning of the group sessions, consequences that will occur if confidentiality is broken. A logical consequence would be that Clarissa would no longer be a member of the group. The reason for this consequence can be explained by telling the students that when personal things are told outside the group, it is difficult to restore the group's trust level. It is even more difficult to do this if the outspoken student is still a member of the group. To save the group, in other words, it is necessary to eliminate the student who could destroy it.

The counselor could be in a difficult situation if Clarissa denied that she broke confidentiality. If this happens, the counselor must speak with Clarissa by herself. Before this individual session, it is important for the counselor to determine, if possible, whether the incident actually happened the way it was reported.

What can you do when the group's composition prevents progress?

Mr. Adams, the school counselor, works with a group of boys who have behavior problems. They are all from the same class and have known each other for a number of years. Whenever the group is in session, Mr. Adams spends a great deal of time telling the boys to correct their behavior so the group can continue.

There are times when group composition prevents progress. No matter what the counselor tries, the group is just not cohesive. This can happen when the members of the group know each other very well or when the group members lack leadership strength. One way to prevent this problem is to scrutinize each student before setting up the group. Check to see whether the potential group members play with each other at recess, participate in the same outside activities, have been in classes together before, or live in the same neighborhood. If two or more of these conditions exist, it is probably not a good idea to put these students together in a group.

If the problem takes shape after the group is formed, the counselor should try to add new members and form two groups. This allows the counselor to select students who have not had as much contact with the other members. If the group cannot be split, the counselor may have to either terminate the group or complete the contracted number of sessions, realizing that changes will be minimal or nonexistent.

What can you do if group members are not making behavior changes?

Each week, the counselor talks with the group about ways to make friends. The students verbalize what they must do and say they will try to do better when they return to their classes. When the counselor checks with the teachers, she learns that the students are still not doing any better.

Sometimes counselors must be more direct when discussing expectations for behavior change. Young students need specific, concrete directions to follow. Identify the expected behavior change, decide upon a method for making the change, and regularly evaluate the students' progress. Each student must know exactly what change he/she needs to make. Once the change is identified, the counselor should help the student outline a step-by-step procedure for implementing the change. One method of evaluation is to provide the classroom teacher with a simple fill-in form on which to indicate whether the contracted behavior took place during the time noted. A sample form would be:

> *Louise Parker* will not bother any students at the water fountain during the week of *October 5*.
>
> Signed
> *Louise Parker*
>
> *Louise* did/did not fulfill the behavior contract.
>
> Signed
> *Mrs. Spencer*

What do you do when the group is not cohesive?

Mrs. Zee had planned the group session carefully. Moments after the session started, the students began to whisper, wiggle, and giggle. Once one student started, the rest followed. Mrs. Zee had to continually remind them to settle down and think about what they were supposed to be doing.

Know your group members. Counselors who know their group members and how they behave in class will be better able to plan their group sessions. A brief conference with the classroom teacher before group sessions begin will provide this information.

A 30-minute discussion period is as much of an eternity for a group of restless students as a 30-minute classroom work period. If the classroom teacher discussed this problem with the counselor, the counselor would suggest that the teacher vary the activities. The counselor should do the same. Restless students need variety. Divide the counseling session time into two or three activities related to the group's purpose. If you do, students will be better able to pay attention and to learn what is expected of them.

GROUPS TO GO: SMALL GROUPS FOR COUNSELORS ON THE GO © 2006 MAR✶CO PRODUCTS, INC. 1-800-448-2197

What can you do when you lose control?

Each session is a hassle. The group enters the room and refuses to do what the counselor has planned. Sometimes the students convince the counselor to change his plans and let them talk about what they want. Sometimes they make fun of what they are to do by telling the counselor the activity is for "babies." They sabotage the group each week and the counselor feels completely at their mercy.

Should this group *be* a group? There are times when students referred for group counseling truly do not want to be there. If their desire to get out is strong enough, they will do almost anything to get their wish. Admit defeat. By honestly admitting to the students that their lack of cooperation is defeating the group's purpose, you will not be telling them anything they do not know. You will only be letting them know you are aware of the situation. Students who want control respond when given control. So the counselor must allow the students to share in the group's decisions and administration.

Begin by asking the group members if they want the sessions to continue. If they do not, disband the group and work with the students individually or through the classroom teacher. If the students want to continue, tell them that everyone must work together to fulfill the group's purpose. Together, set goals for the group, rules, and consequences. By allowing the students to decide whether to participate in the group, you have given them some control over its continuance or termination. By allowing the students to help set the goals, rules, and consequences, you have given them some control over the group's administration. Students who participate in setting goals, rules, and consequences feel they have a part in the group's functioning and will respond in a more positive way. If some students want to leave and others want to stay, keep those who want to be involved and work with them on setting the group standards. Let the others leave. Don't make continuance or termination of the group dependent upon a majority vote. Doing so takes away the individual control that is important to each student.

What can you do when the group doesn't trust the leader?

The counselor has coffee with the classroom teachers every day. They meet in a small, open area outside the classrooms, so the students see them together. Students who see the teachers and counselor together lose confidence in the counselor and ask if he tells the teachers what they have told him.

Counselors must have contact with teachers. That is not only because teachers are professional peers and provide daily adult contact, but because consulting with teachers is part of a counselor's job description. Students sometimes worry about conversations counselors have with teachers, especially if they have told the counselor something they do not want the teacher to know. This puts the counselor in a difficult position, because teacher contact is essential. So is students' trust.

Include a discussion of the meaning of mutual trust as part of an initial group session. You will trust the students, and you expect they will trust you unless you show them they cannot. Explain that having trust in oneself and in others is a part of everyday living and that, without trust, society could not exist. Give examples of what could happen if people did not have faith in others. If no one had faith in a pilot,

GROUPS TO GO: SMALL GROUPS FOR COUNSELORS ON THE GO © 2006 MAR*CO PRODUCTS, INC. 1-800-448-2197

no one would fly in an airplane. If no one had faith in a doctor, no one would go to a hospital. If no one had faith in people, no one would have any friends.

When the group discusses *confidentiality*, counselors should mention their role pertaining to it. Students appreciate honesty. Tell the students that they will see you with the teachers and tell them what you talk about with the teachers. If coffee time is when you talk about your personal life, say so. If you are consulting with a teacher about a member of the group, explain that doing so is part of your job. Emphasize that you will never reveal anything during your consultations that the students have told you in confidence unless you would be breaking the law by not telling an authority.

Now … Go forward!

Use the included groups as presented or adapt them to meet your needs.

ACADEMIC IMPROVEMENT

Time Management

Underachieving Students

TIME MANAGEMENT
(Grades 3-5)

Incomplete assignments cause many different problems. Grades fall, parents become upset, students lose confidence in themselves, and teachers become frustrated. The reason for this problem is usually the student's inability to use time properly. For years, report cards have included a place for teachers to evaluate their students' use of time. Some students receive less than satisfactory marks in that space year after year after year. Counselors can address this problem by offering short, small-group sessions on the use of time for students needing help with this skill.

The demands of modern-day education are increasing. There is more to learn each year and no more time in which to learn the required information. So older students must think constructively about their use of time.

This group is designed to help students:

- Recognize "time-wasters"
- Understand the importance of time management
- Make a workable personal schedule

Group candidates:

- Students who repeatedly do not complete work
- Students who repeatedly turn in incomplete work
- Six to eight students from the same or adjoining grade levels

Group preparation:

Interview each student selected individually and explain the purpose and process of the group. Then send a parent notification and permission letter (page 19).

Dear _____,

Managing time effectively is an essential lifeskill. Children your son or daughter's age who do not manage time effectively have difficulty feeling a sense of accomplishment. That is because they often fail to turn in assignments or those assignments they do turn in may not be completed to the best of the student's ability.

Your child's classroom teacher has identified your child as a student who could benefit from extra help in time management.

In an effort to help your child and others learn more about time management, I am forming a counseling group that will focus on helping children understand the importance of making a daily schedule and not wasting time.

There will be four group meetings scheduled at a time the classroom teacher selects.

Your child knows about the group and has indicated that he or she would like to participate. However, no child is ever included in a small-group counseling program without his or her parents' knowledge and permission.

Please indicate, by completing the form below, that you wish to have your child participate in this group or that you do not want him or her to be included.

Return the permission slip to me by _____.

Thank you,

✂ -

☐ I, _____, *give permission* for my child to participate in the small-group counseling program on time management.

☐ I, _____, *do not give permission* for my child to participate in the small-group counseling program on time management.

Child's Name _____   Date _____

School_____   Grade_____

Teacher _____

Home Phone (_____) _____   Work Phone (_____) _____

Parent's Printed Name _____

Parent's Signature _____

Session 1
TIME-WASTERS

Objective:

To identify ways students waste time and acknowledge personal "time-wasters"

Materials Needed:

For each student:
☑ Piece of art paper
☑ Crayons or markers

For the leader:
☑ Tape

Session Preparation:

Gather the necessary materials.

Session:

• Begin the group by asking the students the following questions:

  What is time?

  Why is time important?

• Distribute a piece of art paper and markers or crayons to each student. Ask the students to think of "Time-Wasters" and draw a picture of what they feel is the greatest student time-waster.

• Give the students enough time to finish their pictures. Then discuss the drawings.

• Hang the drawings somewhere in the room where they are visible to the group. Then ask the following question:

  Why do students have "Time-Waster" problems?

• Conclude the session by discussing why students waste time. Ask the students to name the ways they are most likely to waste time.

CHOICES AND CONSEQUENCES

Objective:

To have the students make decisions about things that are important to them and analyze the consequences for each decision

Materials Needed:

For each student:
- ☑ Copy of *Choices And Consequences* (page 22)
- ☑ Pencil

For the leader:
- ☐ None

Session Preparation:

Reproduce *Choices And Consequences* for each student. Gather any other necessary materials.

Session:

- Distribute *Choices And Consequences* and a pencil to each student.

- Ask the students to think about what they want to do each day (eat, play with friends, watch TV, do homework, etc.). Tell them to select one thing from their list that is really important to them and write it in the first column.

- Have the students write in the second column when they would like to do what they have written in the first column.

- The students should now think about how their choice will benefit them or will be a good thing for them to do. Write that answer in the last column.

- Tell the students to think of nine more things they want to do each day and complete the chart in the same manner.

- Conclude the session by discussing what the students have written on their charts.

- Collect the charts for use in the next session.

CHOICES AND CONSEQUENCES

WHAT I WANT TO DO	WHEN I WANT TO DO IT	WHAT I WILL GAIN

Objective:

To have the students make a daily schedule for everything they want to do

Materials Needed:

For each student:
- ☑ Chart from Session 2
- ☑ Copy of *Time-Management Schedule* (page 24)
- ☑ Pencil

For the leader:
- ☐ None

Session Preparation:

Reproduce *Time-Management Schedule* for each student. Gather any other necessary materials.

Session:

- Distribute the charts from Session 2, *Time-Management Schedule*, and a pencil to each student.

- Explain that the purpose of this session is for the students to learn to fit all the things they want to do each day into the time they have.

- Have the students look at their charts from the previous session and decide how much time they need to do each thing. Then tell them to use the *Time-Management Schedule* and make a schedule for the day, fitting each activity into the time available. Since most things listed will take place before or after school, you may have to tell the students to schedule only those parts of the day.

- Conclude the session by asking the students to answer the following questions:

    Did everything fit easily into the schedule?

    Is there enough time for everything?

- Collect the schedules and the charts. Save them for the final session.

Name_____   Date_____

TIME-MANAGEMENT SCHEDULE

BEFORE SCHOOL:

DURING SCHOOL:

AFTER SCHOOL:

AFTER DINNER:

MAKING A WORKABLE SCHEDULE

Objective:

To design a workable schedule and help the students realize the importance of a workable schedule

Materials Needed:

For each student:
- ☑ Copy of *Time-Management Schedule* (page 24—for students needing to revise their schedules)
- ☑ Pencil (for students needing to revise their schedules)

For the leader:
- ☑ Students' schedules and charts from Session 3

Session Preparation:

Before the session begins, carefully look over the charts and the schedules. Note any times that may be problematic. Reproduce *Time-Management Schedules* for those students needing to revise their schedules. Gather any other necessary materials.

Session:

- Begin the session by asking the following question:

    What would happen if you had not set aside enough time to complete something you wanted to do?

- Tell the students that it is important to prioritize their needs so that they have time to complete the most important tasks.

- Distribute *Time-Management Schedules* and a pencil to those students needing to revise their schedules.

- Refer to the schedules that appear to be problematic. Ask the students, as a group, to reorganize the schedule so it will be workable. Do this by having the students who originally wrote the schedules prioritize the list. Then, with the students, look at the list and adjust the amount of time needed for each activity. Have the select student copy the schedule onto the new *Time-Management Schedule*.

- Conclude the group by telling the students that if they prioritize their activities, make schedules, reorganize schedules when they do not work, and continue to do this until schedules are workable they will be able to manage their time more efficiently.

GROUPS TO GO: SMALL GROUPS FOR COUNSELORS ON THE GO © 2006 MAR★CO PRODUCTS, INC. 1-800-448-2197

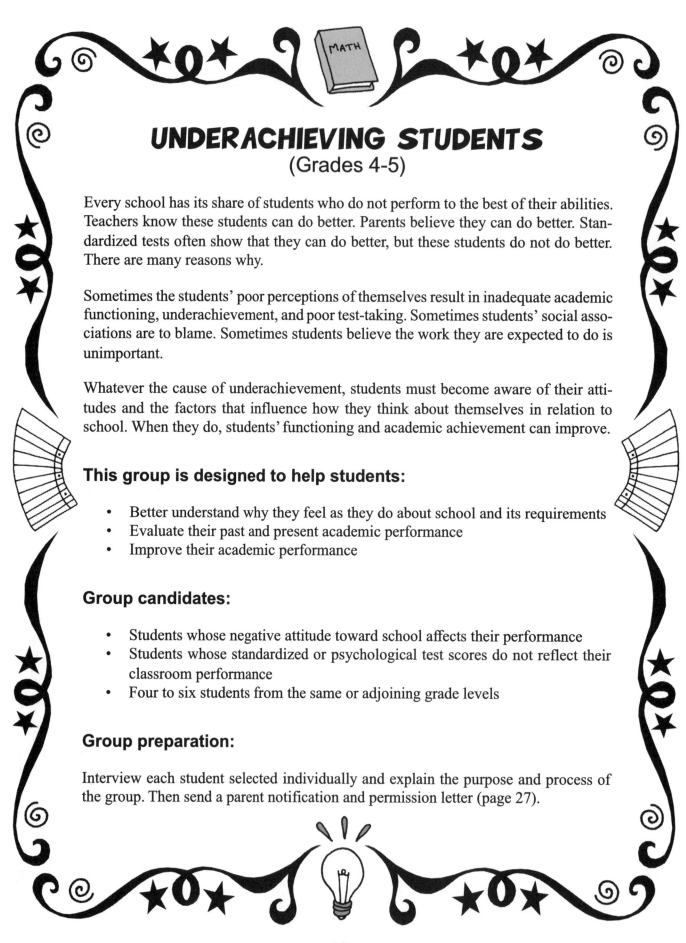

UNDERACHIEVING STUDENTS
(Grades 4-5)

Every school has its share of students who do not perform to the best of their abilities. Teachers know these students can do better. Parents believe they can do better. Standardized tests often show that they can do better, but these students do not do better. There are many reasons why.

Sometimes the students' poor perceptions of themselves result in inadequate academic functioning, underachievement, and poor test-taking. Sometimes students' social associations are to blame. Sometimes students believe the work they are expected to do is unimportant.

Whatever the cause of underachievement, students must become aware of their attitudes and the factors that influence how they think about themselves in relation to school. When they do, students' functioning and academic achievement can improve.

This group is designed to help students:

- Better understand why they feel as they do about school and its requirements
- Evaluate their past and present academic performance
- Improve their academic performance

Group candidates:

- Students whose negative attitude toward school affects their performance
- Students whose standardized or psychological test scores do not reflect their classroom performance
- Four to six students from the same or adjoining grade levels

Group preparation:

Interview each student selected individually and explain the purpose and process of the group. Then send a parent notification and permission letter (page 27).

Dear _____,

Every child deserves the opportunity to learn as much as he or she can during his or her school years. Some children do. Others do not. Teachers know and parents believe that these children could do better. Test scores often indicate they have abilities that classroom performance does not reflect.

Your child's classroom teacher has identified your child as a student who does not work up to his or her potential.

In an effort to help your child and others learn more about academic achievement, I am forming a counseling group that will focus on helping children understand why they do not achieve as much as they could and will provide strategies that give them the opportunity to change.

There will be eight group meetings scheduled at a time the classroom teacher selects.

Your child knows about the group and has indicated that he or she would like to participate. However, no child is ever included in a small-group counseling program without his or her parents' knowledge and permission.

Please indicate, by completing the form below, that you wish to have your child participate in this group or that you do not want him or her to be included.

Return the permission slip to me by _____.

Thank you,

✂ - ✂ - - - - - -

☐ I, _____, *give permission* for my child to participate in the small-group counseling program for academic improvement.

☐ I, _____, *do not give permission* for my child to participate in the small-group counseling program for academic improvement.

Child's Name _____   Date _____

School_____   Grade_____

Teacher _____

Home Phone (_____) _____   Work Phone (_____) _____

Parent's Printed Name _____

Parent's Signature _____

WHAT OR WHO INFLUENCES ATTITUDES ABOUT SCHOOL

Objective:

To identify people and things that influence attitudes about school

Materials Needed:

For each student:
- ☑ Piece of drawing paper
- ☑ Pencil

For the leader:
- ☐ None

Session Preparation:

Gather the necessary materials.

Session:

- Distribute a sheet of drawing paper and a pencil to each student. Ask the students to draw a picture of themselves in the middle of the page. Tell them not to make their drawing too large, as they will be placing other things around their *Self-Picture*. Instruct them to draw a circle around the completed drawing.

- Tell the students that this is their *Circle Of Self,* which contains many different things that affect the way they look at life. By the time the group ends, the students will know a great many things about what their *Circle Of Self* contains and how these things affect what they do.

- Collect the drawings. Tell the students their drawings will be returned to them at a later session.

- Tell the students that they have been selected to be part of this group because people who know and care about them feel they can do better in school. Then ask:

  Who or what do you believe influences kids' attitudes about school? (Friends, teachers, parents, brothers, sisters, past successes or failures in school, etc.)

- Once the students have named all the different influences, ask:

  Do you feel you have a good (positive) attitude or a bad (negative) attitude about school?

- Conclude the session by saying that during the following sessions, the students will have the opportunity to explore their own and other students' feelings about school.

Objective:

To identify how the family values education and how the students' brothers and sisters achieve in the school setting

Materials Needed:

For each student:
- ☑ Piece of lined paper
- ☑ Pencil

For the leader:
- ☐ None

Session Preparation:

Gather the necessary materials.

Session:

- Distribute a piece of lined paper and a pencil to each student. Ask the students to list their family members on the paper. If they feel they know how family members such as grandparents, aunts, uncles, and cousins feel about education, they may also include those people. Have the students record the grade levels of everyone on the list who is still in school.

- Have each student tell why he/she chose to include each person on the list. Make sure the student tells how each person feels about education and what has led the student to that conclusion.

- Have the students look at their lists and respond to the following questions:

    Are most people on your list in higher or lower grades than you? Are you in the highest or lowest grade?

    Do the people on your list who are still in school achieve more, less, or about the same amount as you?

    How does the way these people perform in school influence you?

(*Note:* After the session, you may want to jot down notes about the answers given by the students.)

- Continue the session by asking:

    How do your parents react when you get a good grade in school?

    How do your parents react when you get a poor grade in school?

- Conclude the session by having each student complete the following sentences:

    My parents feel that education is ...

    My brothers and sisters feel that education is ...

    Other members of my family feel that education is ...

    My feelings about education are the same as/different from my family's because I feel ...

MY FRIENDS

Objective:

To identify how the students' friends feel about academic achievement

Materials Needed:

For each student:
- ☑ Piece of lined paper
- ☑ Pencil

For the leader:
- ☑ Chalkboard and chalk or chart paper and marker

Session Preparation:

Gather the necessary materials.

Session:

- Remind the students that, in the last session, they identified how their family felt about education and whether they agreed with that feeling. Tell them that today's session is going to be about their friends and their friends' feelings and behaviors in school.

- Go to the chalkboard/chart paper and write the words: *Bookworm, Nerd, Geek*. Ask the students what they think these words mean and what other words are often used to describe students who do well in school. Then have the students tell why they believe these words are used.

- Distribute a piece of lined paper and a pencil to each student. Tell the students to list the names of their friends. If they do not want to list names, tell them to use some kind of code so they will know which friend is which on the list. Tell them they will not be reading these names aloud and they may shred the paper at the end of the session.

- Have the students put a checkmark by each name on their list that represents someone who:

    - Always or almost always turns in homework
    - Finishes class assignments on time
    - Does not have a behavior problem in class or other places in school
    - Gets mostly A's and B's on tests and other graded papers
    - Volunteers to do extra-credit projects
    - If asked privately (not in front of other kids) would most likely say he/she likes school

- Read each statement again and have the students put an "X" beside each statement they would answer "yes" about themselves.

- Ask the students if they feel they are more like or unlike their friends.

- Discuss how their friends' attitudes about doing well or poorly academically affect their own personal achievement.

- Conclude the session by having the students take their papers and write a confidential one-word response to the following:

    My friends' attitude toward school helps or hinders my attitude toward school.

- Have students shred their papers if they desire.

Objective:

To explore how the students believe their teachers feel about them

Materials Needed:

For each student:
- ☑ Piece of drawing paper
- ☑ Pencil

For the leader:
- ☐ None

Session Preparation:

Gather the necessary materials.

Session:

- Review the last two sessions, reminding the students they have learned about how their family and their friends influence how they feel about school. Today, they will be thinking about their teachers.

- Give each student a sheet of drawing paper and a pencil. Tell the students to design the ideal teacher, drawing him/her in the center of their paper and listing, around the sides of the drawing, all the qualities this person should possess.

- When everyone has finished, have the students share their drawings. As the students share their drawings, select some of the qualities mentioned and ask each student why he/she chose that quality. As the students explain their choices, have them explain how each character trait would help students learn.

(*Note:* If any student tests the activity with remarks like "let us play all day," lead the discussion to show how that attitude would harm, rather than help, students. Involve the other students in a way that shows they do not agree with the student making the suggestion.)

- When the students have finished sharing their drawings, have each student look at his/her drawing and answer the following two questions:

  How do you believe your ideal teacher's characteristics relate to your current teacher?

  How do you believe your ideal teacher's characteristics relate to teachers you have had in the past?

- Conclude the session with the following silent-answer questions. Tell the students to answer these questions to themselves.

  Do you believe your teacher affects your attitude toward school?

  Do you believe your attitude toward school affects your teacher?

PAST AND PRESENT ACADEMIC ACHIEVEMENTS

Objective:

To help the students evaluate their past and present academic achievements

Materials Needed:

For each student:
- ☑ Graph paper
- ☑ Pencil
- ☑ Crayons or colored pencils

For the leader:
- ☑ Graph paper
- ☑ Pencil

Session Preparation:

Gather the necessary materials. For demonstration purposes, make a graph according to the activity directions.

Session:

- Tell the students that in this session, they will be looking at their past academic performance and their academic performance at present.

- Distribute graph paper, crayons or colored pencils, and a pencil to each student. Demonstrating, give the following directions:

  Starting at the bottom of the left side of the page, write Kindergarten through

your current grade. Your current grade should be at the bottom of the right side of the page. The other grades should be evenly spaced in between.

Along the left margin, starting at the bottom, mark off every five boxes. Label each level: Poor, Fair, Good, Very Good, Excellent.

- Have the students think about each of the grade levels, beginning with Kindergarten. Have them evaluate how they did academically each year and place a different-colored "X" at the appropriate level for each grade as shown in the diagram below.

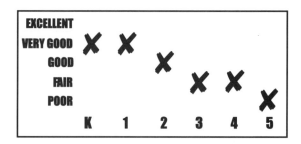

- Once the students have completed this task, ask them to share their graphs and tell the group why they believe there might have been highs or lows at various points in their school career. Tell them they need only share those points they wish to share. They may skip any points they do not care to share.

- Conclude the session by having the students tell what they have learned about the type of situation in which they perform best.

ACHIEVING IN DIFFERENT SUBJECTS

Objective:

To allow the students to evaluate their achievement in each subject they are studying

Materials Needed:

For each student:
- ☑ Piece of graph paper
- ☑ Pencil

For the leader:
- ☑ Piece of graph paper
- ☑ Pencil

Session Preparation:

Gather the necessary materials. Following the session directions, make a graph for demonstration purposes.

Session:

- Distribute graph paper and a pencil to each student.

- Show the students the graph made for demonstration purposes and tell them that in this session, they are going to make a bar graph of all the subject areas they are studying. Ask the students to name each of the subjects they study and, as they do, list each subject (see diagram). They will probably list math, English, reading, social studies, science, art, music, and gym.

- Beginning at the bottom on left side of the page, have the students write the following words five spaces apart: *Terrible, Pretty Good, Good, Very Good,* and *Excellent.*

- Show the students how to make a bar graph for each subject, stopping at the level they feel is appropriate for their achievement in that subject (see diagram below).

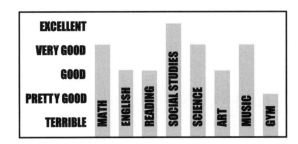

- When the students have completed the bar graphs, have them share their graphs and tell why they believe they perform better in some areas than in others.

- Conclude the session by having each student tell whether liking a particular subject affects his/her performance or if doing well affects how he/she feels about a particular subject.

GROUPS TO GO: SMALL GROUPS FOR COUNSELORS ON THE GO © 2006 MAR★CO PRODUCTS, INC. 1-800-448-2197

EVALUATING INFLUENCES ON SCHOOL ACHIEVEMENT

Objective:

To encourage the students to relate the different influences discussed to their personal lives

Materials Needed:

For each student:
- ☑ *Self-Picture* from Session 1
- ☑ Pencil

For the leader:
- ☐ None

Session Preparation:

Gather the necessary materials.

Session:

- Review the previous five sessions, emphasizing the influences (family, friends, brothers and sisters, extended family members, teachers, past academic performance, liking subjects, etc.) each session discussed.

- Return the *Self-Pictures* drawn in Session 1 and distribute a pencil to each student. Tell the students to think about each of these influences and draw a circle for each one they believe affects the way they think about school. The circles should be drawn according to the greater or lesser influence each influence has. Tell the children to label the influence for each circle and write major influences on the large circles, minor influences on the small circles, etc.

- Ask the students to draw arrows from the circles to their *Self-Picture* and place on each line a positive or negative sign (+ or –) indicating the kind of influence each factor has on them.

- Conclude the session by discussing how the various attitudes and factors affect each individual's attitudes toward achievement in school.

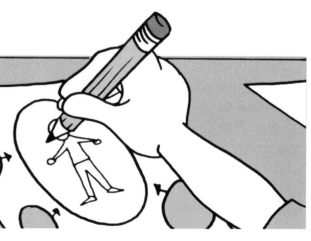

34

COMMITMENT TO CHANGE

Objective:

To encourage the students to make a commitment to change

Materials Needed:

For each student:
- ☑ Copy of *Contract For Change* (page 36)
- ☑ Paper
- ☑ Pencil

For the leader:
- ☐ None

Session Preparation:

Reproduce *Contract For Change* for each student. Gather any other necessary materials.

Session:

- Distribute paper and a pencil to each student. Have the students write an "I learned" statement about themselves.

- Have the students read their statements, then ask them to consider how they might improve their academic progress.

- As the students discuss changes they could make, ask them to decide whether they are willing to make the necessary commitment.

- Distribute *Contract For Change* to each student willing to make a commitment. Have the students complete and sign the contract specifying what they are willing to do to improve their academic performance. The counselor should also sign the contract.

- Conclude the session by having the students take their contracts to their teachers to have them witness the contract. Explain that contracts sometimes need to be revised and that if any student and his/her teacher think revision is necessary, the contract will be rewritten to help further their academic improvement.

  (*Note:* A time may be arranged to evaluate the success of the contract with the student and and/or teacher.)

CONTRACT FOR CHANGE

I _____

WILL _____

_____

_____

_____

_____

_____

SIGNED _____

WITNESS COUNSELOR _____

WITNESS TEACHER _____

36

AT-RISK BEHAVIORS

Uncooperative Behavior

Stress

UNCOOPERATIVE BEHAVIOR
(Grades 3-5)

Lack of cooperation is one of the behaviors most noticeable in disruptive students. These students want things their way and they want to be in control. They demonstrate uncooperative behavior in the classroom by being argumentative and spend much of their time calling attention to themselves in negative ways. If this behavior is allowed to continue, these children will find themselves without friends. As they grow older, they will lack the skills needed to be successful in the world of work and in personal relationships.

This group is designed to help students:

- Realize how their behaviors make others feel and how they themselves feel when others make them the object of the same behaviors
- Appreciate the need to change their behavior

Group candidates:

- Students who display disruptive behaviors in the classroom
- Four to six students from the same grade level

Group preparation:

Interview each student selected individually and explain the purpose and process of the group. Then send a parent notification and permission letter (page 39).

GROUPS TO GO: SMALL GROUPS FOR COUNSELORS ON THE GO © 2006 MAR✱CO PRODUCTS, INC. 1-800-448-2197

Dear _____,

Every child deserves the opportunity to learn as much as he or she can during his or her school years. When a classroom is disrupted by a student whose behavior makes it difficult or impossible for others to learn, the entire class suffers. Carried over into adulthood, this type of behavior can create difficulties in the world of work and in personal relationships.

Your child's classroom teacher has identified your child as a student who displays this type of behavior.

In an effort to help your child and others derive more from the school experience, I am forming a counseling group that will focus on helping children understand how this type of behavior affects other children and how it also affects the disruptive student.

There will be six group meetings scheduled at a time the classroom teacher selects.

Your child knows about the group and has indicated that he or she would like to participate. However, no child is ever included in a small-group counseling program without his or her parents' knowledge and permission.

Please indicate, by completing the form below, that you wish to have your child participate in this group or that you do not want him or her to be included.

Return the permission slip to me by _____.

                    Thank you,

✂ -

☐ I, _____, *give permission* for my child
to participate in the small-group counseling program on cooperation.
☐ I, _____, *do not give permission* for my
child to participate in the small-group counseling program on cooperation.

Child's Name _____   Date _____

School _____   Grade _____

Teacher _____

Home Phone (_____) _____   Work Phone (_____) _____

Parent's Printed Name _____

Parent's Signature _____

39

Objective:

To allow the students to experience their first co-operative project

Materials Needed:

For each student:
☐ None

For the leader:
☑ Sheet of brown mural paper
☑ Box of crayons or markers
☑ Chalkboard and chalk or
   chart paper and marker
☑ Tape
☑ Table and chairs

Session Preparation:

Place the mural paper and crayons or markers in the center of a table. Place chairs for the students around the table. Gather any other necessary materials.

Session:

* Have the students seat themselves around the table and introduce themselves by giving their name and naming one thing they do not like someone to do to them.

* Tell the students that they will be working together for the next six weeks to learn about how and why people behave the way they do.

* Add that spending time together for the next six weeks will be like being in a club. Since the students are like members of a club, they should choose a name for their group and design a group flag. The flag may be designed in any way as long as everyone has a say in choosing the design and an opportunity to work on the flag.

* Tell the students how much time they have to discuss and decide on a name. Begin by writing all the suggestions on the board/chart paper. Eliminate suggested names one by one until only a few are left. Then have the students vote. The vote may be secret or open.

* Tell the students how much time they have to design and create the flag. (Expect this to be difficult, as it will be the students' first cooperative venture and everyone will probably have his/her own ideas. Let them work it out, no matter how disorganized the final product may be.)

* Once the flag is completed, hang it in a place where it can remain until the group disbands.

* Ask the students to look at their flag. Then ask:

  What do you think of your flag?

  Was making the flag easy or hard?

* Conclude the session by having each student tell what could have made the flag better. (Expect the students to say that if others had listened to their ideas, the flag would have been better. Be prepared for blaming.) When the allotted time has elapsed, tell the students to return to their classrooms. (It is likely that no agreement will have been reached.)

GROUPS TO GO: SMALL GROUPS FOR COUNSELORS ON THE GO © 2006 MAR*CO PRODUCTS, INC. 1-800-448-2197

Session 2
COOPERATIVE PAINTING

Objective:

To have the students experience cooperative painting in which everyone contributes to everyone else's work

Materials Needed:

For each student:
- ☑ Drawing paper
- ☑ Brush
- ☑ Several shades of tempera paint
- ☑ Paint cups
- ☑ Bowl of water
- ☑ Paper towel

For the leader:
- ☑ CD player and music CD
- ☑ Tape
- ☑ Table and chairs

Session Preparation:

Place a piece of drawing paper and a brush on the table in front of each student's seat. Put several paint cups, tempera paint, a bowl of water, and a paper towel at each student's place. Gather any other necessary materials.

Session:

- Have the students seat themselves around the table.

- Tell the students they may paint anything they wish on their paper while the music is playing. When the music stops, they must take the place of the person on their right. When the music starts again, they are to add to the painting that person has started, continuing to paint until the music stops. When the music stops, each student will take the place of the student on his/her right and begin adding to that painting as soon as the music starts again. Explain that this will continue until each student has added to everyone else's picture. The activity will conclude when everyone is back in his/her original place.

- Begin the music. Play it for two to three minutes, then stop. Have the students move and begin again. Continue this process until everyone is back in his/her original seat. (You may notice that the students seem more concerned about what someone is putting on their painting than on what they are doing themselves. If they feel someone is ruining their painting, they may become angry and deliberately mess up the painting they are working on. Interfere only as a last resort. Remember: This is a learning experience for the students.)

- When the activity is completed, have the students hang their pictures where they are visible to everyone and clean up their paint area. Then ask:

  How did you feel when someone else painted on your picture?

  How did you feel when you returned to your picture?

  Can you think of another time when you felt like this? (You may hear responses such as when someone called someone a name, someone fought with them, someone destroyed something of theirs, etc.)

41

How did you feel when you painted on other students' pictures? (You may hear the response that they wanted to get even for what was being done to their pictures.)

Did the way you felt make you feel good? (Most will say they didn't like their angry feelings.)

- Guide the discussion toward how this activity and the feelings derived from it relate to various classroom situations. Focus especially on disruptive behaviors.

- Conclude the session by telling the students how changes in their behavior might affect how others feel about them and act toward them.

Session 3
PARTNER PAINTING

Objective:

To allow the students to experience cooperative painting with a partner

Materials Needed:

For each pair of students:
- ☑ 1 piece of drawing paper
- ☑ 2 brushes
- ☑ Several shades of tempera paint
- ☑ Paint cups
- ☑ Bowl of water
- ☑ 2 paper towels

For the leader:
- ☑ CD player and music CD
- ☑ Tape
- ☑ Chalkboard and chalk or chart paper and marker
- ☑ Table and chairs

Session Preparation:

Gather the necessary materials.

Session:

- Have the students seat themselves around the table.

- Review the last session. Review the feelings students experienced and encourage them to draw conclusions about why certain things happened. When the fact that they did not cooperate is mentioned, go to the board/chart paper and write *Cooperation* in bold letters. If it is not mentioned, write the word then discuss its meaning and how it relates to what happened in the last session.

- Tell each student to choose a partner with whom he/she will paint a picture. Distribute drawing paper, two brushes, paint cups, tempera paint, a bowl of water, and two paper towels to each partnership. Explain that the students will have five minutes to draw anything they like, but that they may not communicate verbally.

- Begin playing the music and tell the students to begin painting their pictures. When the allotted time has elapsed, have the students hang their pictures where they are visible to everyone, clean up their paint area, then return to their seats.

- Ask the following questions:

  What do you think of your picture today?

  How did you feel when working on these pictures?

  Did you feel the same way during the last session? (The students may say there were not as many angry feelings, the group was calmer, and they were more pleased with their pictures.)

  What made the difference? (Everyone cooperated.)

- Discuss how cooperating in the group and cooperating in the classroom are related. Emphasize that when the students cooperate in the classroom they will achieve the same results as when they cooperated in the group, a more peaceful and calmer environment.

- Conclude the session by congratulating the students on the behavior change they showed in the activity and encourage them to carry this behavior over into their classrooms.

43

COOPERATING AS A GROUP, AGAIN

Objective:

To allow the students to experience, for the second time, cooperating as a group

Materials Needed:

For student:
☑ Paper towel
☑ Different colors of clay

For the leader:
☑ CD player and music CD
☑ Tape
☑ Chalkboard and chalk or chart paper and marker
☑ Table and chairs

Session Preparation:

Place a paper towel and different colors of clay in front of each student's seat. Gather any other necessary materials.

Session:

(**Note:** This session uses the same concepts, format, and discussion questions as Session 2. Only the medium has changed. Instead of paint, the students will work with clay. The purpose of this session is to monitor the students' cooperative behavior in a similar situation.)

• Have the students seat themselves around the table.

• Tell the students that they are going to work with clay and may make anything they like with the clay while the music is playing. Their project will be like a sculpture. When the music stops, they will move to the right and work on that student's sculpture until the music stops. Each time the music stops, each student will again move to the right. Explain that this will continue until each student has moved and contributed to each sculpture. The activity will stop when everyone is back in his/her original seat. Tell the students that during this activity, they may talk among themselves.

• Play the music for two to three minutes, then stop. Have the students move and begin again. Continue until everyone is back in his/her original seat. (You may notice that although some tempers may flare, the intensity of anger is less than in the previous session and the students are more concerned about how the originator of the project is going to feel about what has been added to his/her sculpture. You may also notice such questions as "What do you think of this?" "Is this the way you want it?" and "What color clay did you want?")

• When the activity is completed, ask:

How did you feel when someone else worked on your sculpture?

How did you feel when you returned to your sculpture?

How did you feel when you worked on someone else's sculpture? (Look for responses such as concern for the original sculptor, being less angry, and planning what to do before actually doing it.)

Did the caring about the design of other students' sculptures make you feel good?

- Guide the discussion toward how this activity and the feelings derived from it differ from those in Session 2.

- Have the students clean up their work area.

- Conclude the session by congratulating the students on being more cooperative and considerate. Re-emphasize the difference this behavior will make in their classroom and in other students' opinions of them.

Objective:

To allow the students to experience cooperative sculpting with a partner

Materials Needed:

For each pair of students:
- ☑ Different colors of clay
- ☑ Paper towel

For the leader:
- ☑ CD player and music CD
- ☑ Table and chairs

Session Preparation:

Gather the necessary materials.

Session:

(*Note:* This session uses the same concepts, format, and discussion questions as Session 3. Only the medium has changed. Instead of paint, the students will work with clay. The purpose of this session is to monitor the students' cooperative behavior in a similar situation.)

- Have the students seat themselves around the table.

- Review the previous session. Review the feelings the students experienced and encourage them to draw conclusions about why certain feelings occurred. Compliment each behavior change that the students notice and emphasize that these changes will make their classroom a better place for learning and that they will gain their classmates' respect.

- Tell each student to choose a partner with whom he/she will sculpt a picture out of clay. The picture may have many parts and should tell a story. Give each partnership clay and a paper towel on which to put the clay. Tell the students that they will have five minutes to create anything they like and that they may talk with one another.

- Begin playing the music and have the students begin creating their pictures. When the allotted time has elapsed, have the students tell the story their sculptures depict.

- Then ask the following questions:

  What do you think of your sculpture?

  How did you feel when working on this project?

  Did you feel the same way the last time you worked with a partner?

  What made the difference? (Everyone worked together.)

  How does cooperating affect the feelings you have for others? (When you cooperate, you care about the other person's feelings, you are not trying to have everything your own way, you understand that the other person may have some good ideas, too, etc.)

  How does cooperating affect the feelings others have for you? (When you cooperate, other people will like you and want to do things with you.)

- Conclude the session by congratulating the students on their insightful comments they have made about the importance of cooperation.

CONCLUSION

Objective:

To have the students create a group mural showing what they have learned in the previous sessions

Materials Needed:

For each student:
- ☐ None

For the leader:
- ☑ Large piece of brown mural paper
- ☑ Crayons, pencils, markers
- ☑ Table and chairs

Session Preparation:

Gather the necessary materials. Place the mural paper and the crayons, markers, and pencils on the table.

Session:

- Have the students seat themselves around the table.

- Ask the students the following questions:

  In the first session, we named our group and drew a flag. What do you remember about that session?

  In the second session, we did cooperative painting. What do you remember about that session?

  In the third session, we did partner painting. What do you remember about that session?

  In the fourth session, we did group sculpting with clay. What do you remember about that session?

  In our last session, we did partner sculpting with clay. What do you remember about that session?

- Today, as our final activity, you are to think about what you need to do to work together to draw a group mural. The mural will show, in any way you wish, what you have learned or experienced during our group sessions. When you have finished, give your mural the name you chose for your group in Session 1. (The students may talk about possibilities. Once an agreement has been reached, each student will take a part of the mural to work on.)

- Conclude the group by having the students describe their mural. Thank the students for their cooperation. Encourage them to remember how well they have learned to cooperate, how well cooperation has worked in group, and that it will also work that well in their classrooms.

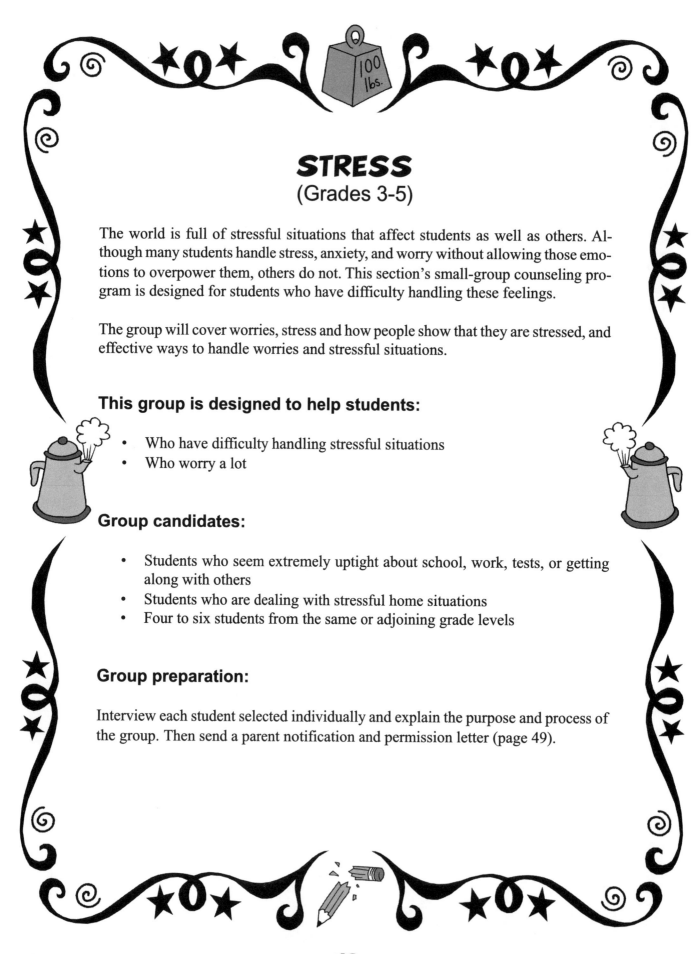

STRESS
(Grades 3-5)

The world is full of stressful situations that affect students as well as others. Although many students handle stress, anxiety, and worry without allowing those emotions to overpower them, others do not. This section's small-group counseling program is designed for students who have difficulty handling these feelings.

The group will cover worries, stress and how people show that they are stressed, and effective ways to handle worries and stressful situations.

This group is designed to help students:

- Who have difficulty handling stressful situations
- Who worry a lot

Group candidates:

- Students who seem extremely uptight about school, work, tests, or getting along with others
- Students who are dealing with stressful home situations
- Four to six students from the same or adjoining grade levels

Group preparation:

Interview each student selected individually and explain the purpose and process of the group. Then send a parent notification and permission letter (page 49).

Dear _____,

The world is full of stressful situations and students are not exempt from stress. Although some students seem to thrive and grow under stress, others allow stress to overpower them. We often see this in students who seem to be extremely uptight about school, work, tests, or getting along with others. Some students are also dealing with stressful home situations.

Your child's classroom teacher has identified your child as a student who displays this type of behavior.

In an effort to help your child and others, I am forming a counseling group that will focus on helping children understand how to learn to deal with stressful and worrisome situations. The students will explore the causes of their stresses and worries and learn to handle both emotions in effective ways.

There will be six group meetings scheduled at a time the classroom teacher selects.

Your child knows about the group and has indicated that he or she would like to participate. However, no child is ever included in a small-group counseling program without his or her parents' knowledge and permission.

Please indicate, by completing the form below, that you wish to have your child participate in this group or that you do not want him or her to be included.

Return the permission slip to me by _____.

Thank you,

✂ -

☐ I, _____, *give permission* for my child to participate in the small-group counseling program to reduce stress and worrying.

☐ I, _____, *do not give permission* for my child to participate in the small-group counseling program to reduce stress and worrying.

Child's Name _____   Date _____

School _____   Grade _____

Teacher _____

Home Phone (_____) _____   Work Phone (_____) _____

Parent's Printed Name _____

Parent's Signature _____

49

IDENTIFYING STRESSFUL SITUATIONS

Objective:

To help the students get to know one another and identify some stressful situations

Materials Needed:

For each student:
☐ None

For the leader:
☑ Chart paper and marker

Session Preparation:

Gather the necessary materials.

Session:

• Begin the group by telling the students how many sessions there will be and when and where the group will meet.

• Review some basic rules. Emphasize the importance of confidentiality, listening to others, sharing, and not putting each other down.

• Have the students introduce themselves, present a brief synopsis of their lives, and name one thing that makes them nervous. The leader may do this first.

• Tell the students that the purpose of the group is to help them learn to deal with things that worry them and to teach them strategies to handle other stresses, anxieties, and worries that might affect them in the future.

• On the chart paper, write "WHAT IF?" in large letters. Then say:

> *I want you to think of* What If *situations that could cause you stress. For example:*
>
> > *What if you spilled a plate of spaghetti all over yourself in a restaurant?*
> >
> > *What if you always had to be "it" in a game of tag?*
> >
> > *What if you studied really hard for a test and then forgot the answers?*

As the students continue adding to the list, write each contribution on the chart paper.

• After each student has contributed at least one *What If?* to the list, review the list and, with the students, decide what would happen, how the person would feel, and what could be done to make the person feel better about the situation.

• Conclude the group by saying:

> *I want you to be aware, between now and the next session, of any* What Ifs? *that cross your minds. Bring those ideas to our next session so we may add them to the list.*

• Save the list of *What Ifs* for the next session.

REAL VERSUS IMAGINARY SITUATIONS

Objective:

To identify the difference between real and imaginary situations that could worry students

Materials Needed:

For each student:
- ☑ Art paper
- ☑ Crayons or markers

For the leader:
- ☑ *What If?* list from Session 1
- ☑ Chart paper and marker

Session Preparation:

Gather the necessary materials.

Session:

- Begin the session by reviewing the list of *What Ifs?* and have the students share any additional *What Ifs?* they thought of since the last meeting. Add these suggestions to the list and discuss what could happen in each case.

- Discuss *real worries* versus *imaginary worries*. Tell the students that sometimes people worry when they see a scary movie. They know it is pretend while they are watching it, but when they go to bed that night, they worry that what they saw might happen to them. Tell the students that another example of a worry that is not real might be to imagine they are having a spelling test and, although they have studied for the test, they can't remember how to spell any of the words. Tell the students that they might not spell all the words correctly, but if they studied, they will not spell all the words incorrectly.

- Have the students analyze each *What If?* to see if it really could happen or would just be an imagined worry.

- Distribute art paper and crayons or markers to each student. Then give the following directions:

    > *With your crayons/markers title your paper* Imaginary Things That I Might Worry Will Happen To Me. *Draw pictures of as many things as you can that fit into this category.*

- Tell the students how much time they have to complete the activity. When the allotted time has elapsed, conclude the session by having the students share their drawings and explain each worry.

- Collect the drawings.

IDENTIFYING STRESSFUL SITUATIONS THAT CAN AND CANNOT BE CHANGED

Objective:

To identify changeable and non-changeable situations and suggest ways to deal with those that can be changed

Materials Needed:

For each student:
  ☐ None

For the leader:
  ☑ *What If?* list from Session 1
  ☑ Drawings from Session 2
  ☑ Chalkboard and chalk or
     chart paper and markers

Session Preparation:

Gather the necessary materials.

Session:

• Begin the session by asking the students to give personal examples in response to the following questions. Record the students' answers on the chalkboard/chart paper.

    What is stress?

    How do people show they are feeling stress?

• Using the students' examples from the *What If?* list from Session 1 and the drawings from Session 2, have the students sort worries and stress into the following four categories:

1. School and schoolwork
2. Friends and getting along
3. Family and home
4. Death and illness

Record the students' answers on the chalkboard/chart paper.

• Review the categories and, using the students' examples, help the students decide which examples they can actually do something about and which ones they cannot change.

Examples:

    I want to get better grades—can change

    I want my friends to like me—can change

    My dad gets drunk and yells at us—cannot change

    I'm scared my grandma will die—cannot change

• Tell the students that it is important to understand that they must accept and adjust to sources of stress that they cannot change and work on those they can change.

• Have the students pick one worry that can be changed. Then, as a group, work out a way to change the situation. After listening to the suggestions for change, tell the students to try each idea before the next session. Tell the students that at the next session, they will have an opportunity to tell how they worked on lowering their worry and stress level and what the results were. Return the drawings to the students.

• Conclude the session by having the students review the suggestions they will be using.

RELIEVING STRESS THROUGH RELAXATION

Objective:

To teach the students stress-relieving techniques

Materials Needed:

For each student:
☐ None

For the leader:
☐ None

Session Preparation:

None.

Session:

- Begin the session by asking the students how the suggestions from the last session worked to reduce the worry they chose.

- Introduce deep breathing as a technique to help stressful situations. Say:

    1. *I want you to think about a positive thing which gives you a feeling of energy and strength. This could be something you do well like playing an instrument or a sport.* (Allow time for the students to think of a positive thing.)

    2. *While thinking about your positive thing, take a deep breath through your nose and let it out through your mouth. As you let your breath out, imagine all tension, worry, and negative feelings going out of you.* (Allow time for the students to do this.)

    3. *You should now feel more relaxed.*

- Tell the students that sighing deeply is another tension reliever. Explain that sighing deeply increases oxygen flow and lowers stress and can be used when there is not enough time for deep breathing.

- Have the students practice both techniques.

- When it is evident that the students have mastered both techniques, talk about when they feel these techniques would help relieve stress.

- Conclude the session by telling the students to use these techniques and report at the next session on how they worked.

53

RELIEVING STRESS THROUGH VISUALIZATION

Objective:

To teach the students another stress-relieving technique

Materials Needed:

For each student:
- ☑ Art paper
- ☑ Crayons or markers

For the leader:
- ☐ None

Session Preparation:

Gather the necessary materials.

Session:

- Have the students describe their experiences with breathing deeply in stressful situations and how they felt the technique worked.

- Tell the students that they are going to learn another way of relaxing. Say:

  1. *Sit in a comfortable position and close your eyes.*

  2. *Squeeze your feet. Then release your feet as you say to yourself, "Release all the tension from my feet."*

  3. *Squeeze the back of your legs. As you release the squeeze, say to yourself, "Release all the tension from the back of my legs and my feet."*

Continue directing the students to squeeze and release different parts of their bodies until they reach their heads. Be sure to include their stomach, arms, shoulders, face, eyes, and any other part of the body you desire.

Tell the students that their bodies should now be completely relaxed.

While the students are in this relaxed state, have them think of a place where they feel comfortable. (Allow some time for the students to feel relaxed in a comfortable place.)

Now allow them to open their eyes.

- Ask the students how they felt when they were relaxed and in their comfortable places.

- Distribute art paper and crayons or markers and have each student draw a picture of his/her comfortable place. Tell the students to keep the pictures to remind them of their comfortable places after the group sessions have concluded.

- Conclude the session by telling the students to practice the relaxation techniques they learned in this session and the previous session whenever they feel worried or stressful.

REVIEW STRESS-RELIEVING TECHNIQUES

Objective:

To review the stress-relieving techniques

Materials Needed:

For each student:
☐ None

For the leader:
☐ None

Session Preparation:

None.

Session:

- Have the students share examples of times they used their relaxation and visualization techniques.

- Review what the students learned in the previous five sessions. Have the students recall the worries or stresses they felt at the beginning of the group sessions and tell how they feel about each one at this time.

- Review each of the techniques presented, making sure that each group member understands how to use deep breathing, sighing, relaxation, and visualization techniques.

- Have each child complete the following two sentences:

    When I feel worried or stressful, I can …

    This group has taught me …

- Conclude the session by thanking the students for their participation and encouraging them to use the techniques presented whenever they feel worried or stressed.

55

DECISION MAKING

Developing Decision-Making Skills

Peer Pressure

LET'S DEVELOP DECISION-MAKING SKILLS
(Grades 4-5)

Students must make many decisions every day, but few realize that they are even making them. Some routine decisions involve what to wear, personal hygiene, what to eat, which friends to choose, etc. The decisions students make affect both academic progress and social relationships. Students who do not make good decisions as they are growing up are more likely not to make good decisions concerning friends, careers, and personal relationships as adults.

This group is designed to help students:

- Recognize what decisions they make
- Understand why they make certain decisions
- Identify alternatives they may use

Group candidates:

- Students who have problems making good decisions
- Students who don't seem to have problems with decision-making but need help clarifying and understanding the process involved in making well-informed decisions about themselves, their education, and their future
- Six to eight students from the same or adjoining grade levels

Group preparation:

Interview each student selected individually and explain the purpose and process of the group. Then send a parent notification and permission letter (page 59).

Dear _____,

Good decision-making skills are a foundation for successful living. Some decisions are made almost without thinking, like what to eat and what to wear. Others—such as whether or not to follow the crowd, the importance of a good attitude in school, and doing homework—are more complicated. Whatever the decision to be made, students must learn to analyze the consequences and remember that they are responsible for whatever choices they make.

Your child's classroom teacher has identified your child as a student who could benefit from extra help in decision making.

In an effort to help your child and others learn more about decision making, I am forming a counseling group that will focus on helping children understand the importance of thinking about alternatives and consequences when faced with making a decision. The students will explore all aspects of decision making.

There will be six group meetings scheduled at a time the classroom teacher selects.

Your child knows about the group and has indicated that he or she would like to participate. However, no child is ever included in a small-group counseling program without his or her parents' knowledge and permission.

Please indicate, by completing the form below, that you wish to have your child participate in this group or that you do not want him or her to be included.

Return the permission slip to me by _____.

Thank you,

✂ -

☐ I, _____, *give permission* for my child to partici-
pate in the small-group counseling program for improvement of decision-making skills.

☐ I, _____, *do not give permission* for my child to
participate in the small-group counseling program for improvement of decision-making skills.

Child's Name _____   Date _____

School _____   Grade _____

Teacher _____

Home Phone (_____) _____   Work Phone (_____) _____

Parent's Printed Name _____

Parent's Signature _____

59

Session 1
DECISIONS EVERYONE MAKES

Objective:

To help students realize the multitude of decisions they make each day

Materials Needed:

For each student:
- ☑ Paper
- ☑ Pencil

For the leader:
- ☐ None

Session Preparation:

Gather the necessary materials.

Session:

- Begin the group by telling the students the nature and purpose of the group, how many sessions there will be, and when and where the group will meet.

- Review some basic rules. Emphasize the importance of confidentiality, listening to others, sharing, and not putting each other down.

- Distribute paper and pencil to each student. Have the students number their papers from 1 to 15. Then ask them to write after each number a description of a decision they made during the previous 24 hours.

 (*Note:* If the group needs further help, get the students started by briefly discussing a few of the decisions students make each morning before school.)

- Have the students share their lists, comparing similarities and differences.

- After everyone has shared his/her list, direct the students to put a star by the five decisions they felt were most important on their lists.

- Have the students number their paper from 1 to 5 and list five decisions they made in the previous month. Have the students share these lists and put stars next to the two decisions they feel were most important.

- Finally, have the students number their paper from 1 to 3 and list the three most important decisions they have made in the previous year. When everyone has finished, have the students share these with the group.

- Conclude the session by reminding the students of the many decisions they make and the importance of making each decision good and positive.

GROUPS TO GO: SMALL GROUPS FOR COUNSELORS ON THE GO © 2006 MAR*CO PRODUCTS, INC. 1-800-448-2197

PERSONAL VALUES AFFECT DECISIONS

Objective:

To help students understand how personal values relate to the decision-making process

Materials Needed:

For each student:
- ☑ Paper
- ☑ Pencil

For the leader:
- ☐ None

Session Preparation:

Gather the necessary materials.

Session:

- Review Session 1 by reminding the students of the many decisions they make each day. Have each student name a decision that he/she felt was very important.

- Introduce the concept of *setting goals*. Ask the students to tell you what they believe *setting goals* means. (It is the step-by-step process of accomplishing a task.)

- Tell the students that *values* are beliefs that people live by and everyone has them. For example, a law-abiding person could feel that breaking the law is wrong. A person might never cheat because he/she feels that cheating is wrong. Being law-abiding and not cheating are values. Have the students name some values they or their families have.

- Explain that students this age are sometimes unsure of their values. This is because values often change as people get older. A younger person may not see the value of attending school regularly, for example, but realize as he/she gets older that not attending school regularly affects how much he/she learns, which affects the grade he/she earns. That, in later life, affects a job he/she might want to have. The value of attending school regularly has then changed for that person.

- Read the following story to the students. Tell them to listen carefully so that when the story is finished, they can name some of Archibald's values and describe how his values affect the decisions he makes.

    During his fourth-grade year, Archibald made a lot of decisions. He thought about some before he made them. He made some decisions without thinking.

    Archibald chose to join a Little League team and worked hard to improve his batting and catching. He put so much time into practice, he did not have much time left over, so he didn't spend much time on his homework. Some of his friends were joining Scouts, so Archibald decided to join, too. But he missed a lot of the meetings.

    When Archibald was absent from school, he played computer games or watched game shows on TV. He did just enough schoolwork to pass each class. Each class, that is, except math. That was a total disaster!

Archibald had a group of friends he hung around with at school and did things with on the weekends. He and his friends went to the movies, bowled, and had sleepovers almost every Friday night.

Archibald got along well with his older sister, who was in high school. But he got into a lot of fights with his younger brother, who was in second grade. Archibald could talk with his mother, but usually disagreed with his father. Archibald's parents want him to go to a good college, but his grades are C's or lower.

• Ask the students what values Archibald has and how these values are affecting the decisions he makes.

• Distribute paper and pencil to each student. Ask the students to quickly list 20 things they like to do. When everyone has done this, have the students:

    1. Put "FA" after each thing they do with their family.

    2. Put "FR" after each thing they do with a friend.

    3. Put $ after each thing that costs more than $5.00.

    4. Put #1 after each thing they do at least once each day.

    5. Put #2 after each thing they do at least once a week.

Have the students total the number of things they listed in each category.

• Conclude the lesson by telling the students to look carefully at their lists, then complete the following sentences aloud.

    Something I learned about myself from the answers on my list is …

    Something surprising that I learned from the answers on my list is …

    Looking at my list, I believe three of my values are …

GROUPS TO GO: SMALL GROUPS FOR COUNSELORS ON THE GO © 2006 MAR*CO PRODUCTS, INC. 1-800-448-2197

IDENTIFYING DECISION-MAKING ALTERNATIVES

Objective:

To help students learn about decision-making alternatives and understand ways to use these alternatives to make good decisions

Materials Needed:

For each student:
- ☐ None

For the leader:
- ☑ Chart paper and marker
- ☑ Tape

Session Preparation:

Label the chart paper *Four Steps For Decision Making*, then add the following:

Step 1—Define the decision and specify when it must be made.

Step 2—List known alternatives.

Step 3—Identify other possible alternatives.

Step 4—Add new alternatives to the list.

Post the chart where all the students can see it.

Session:

- Review, as a group, how personal values affect decision making.

- Write the word *alternatives* on the chart paper. Introduce the concept of *alternatives* by telling the students that *alternatives* are choices made at certain times during the decision-making process. Emphasize that unless alternatives exist there can be no decisions.

- Draw two lines from the word *alternatives*. At the end of one line, write the word *known*. At the end of the other line, write the word *unknown*. Then explain that there are two kinds of alternatives: *known alternatives* (which are obvious to the decision maker) and *unknown alternatives* (which are not obvious to the decision maker).

- Referring to the *Four Steps For Decision Making* chart, present and discuss the four steps to decision making.

- As you present the following hypothetical situations, have the students apply the four steps to each situation. Record what they say on the chart paper.

   Situation 1—You are a member of a group assigned to do a project on life in the American colonies.

   Situation 2—You must make a choice to take karate lessons or join a Little League team.

   Situation 3—Your parents do not like your best friend.

   Situation 4—Your friends are exchanging homework answers so each person does not have so much to do. You want to stay friends, but you do not want to cheat.

- Conclude the session by encouraging each group member to apply the four steps to decision making when making a decision between now and the next session. Save the chart of the four steps in decision making for Session 4.

GROUPS TO GO: SMALL GROUPS FOR COUNSELORS ON THE GO © 2006 MAR*CO PRODUCTS, INC. 1-800-448-2197

APPLYING VALUES TO ACCEPTABLE OR UNACCEPTABLE DECISIONS

Objective:

To help students understand that personal values are involved in choosing alternatives

Materials Needed:

For each student:
>   None

For the leader:
>   ☑ Chart paper and marker
>   ☑ Tape
>   ☑ *Four Steps For Decision Making* chart from Session 3

Session Preparation:

Label the chart paper *Four Steps To Determining Acceptable Alternatives*, then add the following:

1.   Your values
2.   Your goals
3.   Unacceptable alternatives
4.   Acceptable alternatives

Post the *Four Steps For Decision Making* chart and the *Four Steps To Determining Acceptable Alternatives* chart where all the students can see them.

Session:

*   Have the students name the decisions they made since the last session and describe how they applied the four steps for decision mak-

ing. As each decision is described, ask the other group members to add alternatives that could have been considered.

*   Ask the students to tell when an alternative is acceptable and when it is unacceptable. (The answers given will relate to each student's personal values. For example, if an alternative to getting a better grade on a test is to look at someone else's paper, honesty is a personal value of a student who would not do that because he/she will not cheat. Be sure the students understand that their own values are part of what makes an alternative acceptable.)

*   Explore this topic by asking the students how society's values are involved in determining acceptable alternatives. Use the example of a driver running a red light. Society says cars must stop at red lights. Most drivers obey this rule because they risk having an accident or getting a ticket if they do not stop. Have the students give a few other examples.

*   Referring to the *Four Steps To Determining Acceptable Alternatives* chart, review the four steps to determining acceptable alternatives. Then use the following example to demonstrate how to use the four steps:

>   Sample situation:

>   Your teacher has just told you that you are failing the grade because you have not turned in your assignments. You do not want to fail.

>   ***Your values:*** Learning, succeeding

>   ***Your goals:*** Passing the grade

Unacceptable alternatives: Do nothing. Get your parents to talk with the teacher.

Acceptable alternatives: Talk with the teacher about making up the work. Do the work and turn it in. Do not neglect any more assignments.

- Present the following situations. Allow the students to practice the four steps to finding acceptable alternatives. Present and discuss each situation before presenting the next one.

Situation 1:

You and your friends are shopping at the mall. Your friends want you to shoplift a CD that none of you has enough money to buy. You want to keep your friends.

Situation 2:

Your mother needs you to baby-sit your little brother for an hour each day after school until she can get home from work. You want to try out for the basketball team. Practice is held each day after school.

- Ask the students to think of a situation and use it to practice the four steps to finding acceptable alternatives.

- Conclude the session by telling the students to practice the four steps to finding acceptable alternatives with any decision they make between now and the next session.

65

EVALUATING ALTERNATIVES

Objective:

To help students understand how and where to find information to help them clarify alternatives and make decisions

Materials Needed:

For each student:
- ☐ None

For the leader:
- ☑ Chart paper and marker
- ☑ *Four Steps To Determining Acceptable Alternatives* chart from Session 4
- ☑ Tape

Session Preparation:

Post the *Four Steps To Determining Acceptable Alternatives* chart where all the students can see it. Gather any other necessary materials.

Session:

- Have the students describe the decisions they made since the last session and tell how they applied the four steps to acceptable alternatives. If any student is having difficulty, allow him/her to use the *Four Steps To Determining Acceptable Alternatives* chart for the explanation.

- Tell the students that in this session, the group will be exploring how and where to find further information to help them make decisions.

- Read the following situation to the group:

  Samantha is trying to decide whether to go to a dance camp or take a trip with her aunt and uncle and cousins.

  Samantha has been taking dance lessons for four years. She is very good, and her teacher thinks she might even become a professional dancer. She loves dancing and has the opportunity to go to a six-week dance camp with other kids who are also good dancers. Her aunt and uncle are taking her cousins on a two-week trip to DisneyWorld. They have invited Samantha to come along. She has never been to DisneyWorld. Since the trip is at the same time as the camp, she cannot do both. She must choose one or the other.

  Samantha needs help thinking through this decision. She wants to get information that will help her, but she does not want anyone to make up her mind for her.

- Write the following questions on the chart paper. Then ask the students the following questions. As they answer, write the answers on the chart paper under each question:

  Who are people Samantha can talk with? (She can talk with her friends, dance teacher, teacher, aunt and uncle, parents, or school counselor.)

  What can Samantha do? (She can read about what she would do at the dance camp and she can read about what she will see at DisneyWorld.)

  What things should Samantha consider? (She should consider what will be the best for her and what she would enjoy more.)

- Ask the students to name some difficult choices kids their age might have to make. Encourage them to describe personal choices they have been or may be faced with. Have students who are willing to share, describe their situation. Then ask the group members to answer the same type of questions asked about Samantha.

- Conclude the session by encouraging the students to ask these types of questions whenever they are faced with a difficult choice.

MAKING GOOD DECISIONS

Objective:

To help students combine every aspect of decision making and be better prepared to use the process in the future

Materials Needed:

For each student:
- ☑ Copy of *My Thoughts About Decision Making* (page 69)
- ☑ Pencil

For the leader:
- ☑ *Four Steps To Determining Acceptable Alternatives* chart from previous sessions
- ☑ Tape

Session Preparation:

Reproduce *My Thoughts About Decision Making* for each student. Post the *Four Steps To Determining Acceptable Alternatives* chart where all the students can see it.

Session:

- Referring to the *Four Steps To Determining Acceptable Alternatives* chart, review every aspect of decision making that has been discussed. As each topic is discussed, ask the students to explain:

     The meaning of the topic
     How the topic affects decisions making

- Present the following topics:

     Personal values
     Alternatives
     Acceptable and unacceptable alternatives
     Getting further information
     Making a well-informed decision

- Discuss any area in which you feel the students need more understanding.

- Distribute *My Thoughts About Decision Making* and a pencil to each student. Have the students evaluate the group sessions by completing the worksheet.

- Collect the completed worksheets. Thank the students for their participation and encourage them to use what they have learned whenever they must make a decision.

Name_____   Date_____

MY THOUGHTS ABOUT DECISION MAKING

Directions: Please complete the following sentences as honestly as possible.
You may write your name on the paper or leave it blank.

★ Decision making is important because _____

_____

_____

_____ .

★ Something important I learned about decision making is _____

_____

_____

_____ .

★ These sessions have been helpful for me because _____

_____

_____

_____ .

★ If given a choice to participate in another counseling group:

☐ I would like to participate.

☐ I would not like to participate.

69

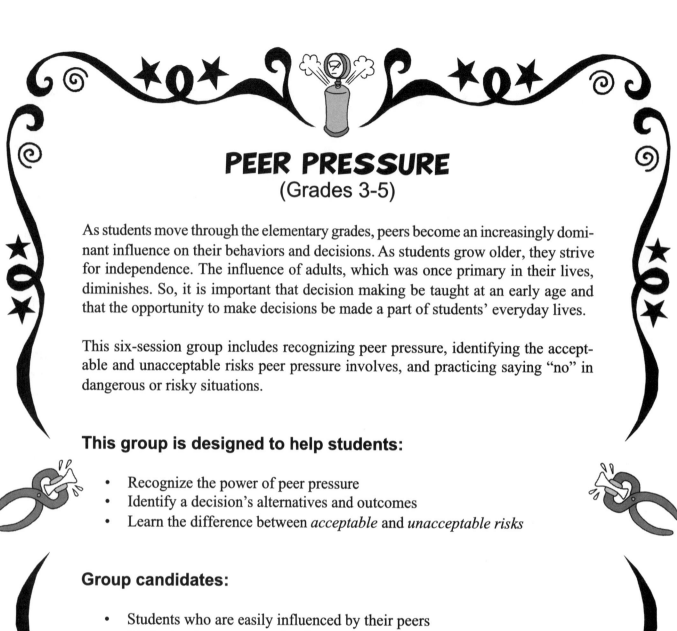

PEER PRESSURE
(Grades 3-5)

As students move through the elementary grades, peers become an increasingly dominant influence on their behaviors and decisions. As students grow older, they strive for independence. The influence of adults, which was once primary in their lives, diminishes. So, it is important that decision making be taught at an early age and that the opportunity to make decisions be made a part of students' everyday lives.

This six-session group includes recognizing peer pressure, identifying the acceptable and unacceptable risks peer pressure involves, and practicing saying "no" in dangerous or risky situations.

This group is designed to help students:

- Recognize the power of peer pressure
- Identify a decision's alternatives and outcomes
- Learn the difference between *acceptable* and *unacceptable risks*

Group candidates:

- Students who are easily influenced by their peers
- Students who seem to strive for peer acceptance
- Six to eight students from the same or adjoining grade levels

Group preparation:

Interview each student selected individually and explain the purpose and process of the group. Then send a parent notification and permission letter (page 71).

Dear _____,

As students move through the elementary grades, peers become a more dominant force in their behaviors and decisions. As students grow older and strive for independence, the adults influence which was once primary in their lives diminishes. Since children will usually be "on their own" when a decision involving peers must be made, it is vital that they recognize peer pressure for what it is and make a decision that is a healthy choice for them.

Your child's classroom teacher has identified your child as a student who could benefit from extra help in making decisions concerning peer pressure.

In an effort to help your child and others learn more about peer pressure, I am forming a counseling group that will focus on helping children understand the importance of thinking about the alternatives and consequences when making a decision. The children will explore all aspects of decision making.

There will be six group meetings scheduled at a time the classroom teacher selects.

Your child is aware of the group and has indicated a desire to participate. However, no child is ever included in a small-group counseling program without his or her parents' knowledge and permission.

Please indicate by completing the form below your wish to have your child take advantage of this opportunity or your wish that he or she not be included.

Return the permission slip to me by _____.

Thank you,

✂ -

☐ I, _____, *give permission* for my child to participate in the small-group counseling program for improvement in making decisions concerning peer pressure.

☐ I, _____, *do not give permission* for my child to participate in the small-group counseling program for improvement in making decisions concerning peer pressure.

Child's Name _____   Date _____

School _____   Grade _____

Teacher _____

Home Phone (____) _____   Work Phone (____) _____

Parent's Printed Name _____

Parent's Signature _____

PEERS CAN AFFECT DECISIONS

Objective:

To introduce the power of peer pressure

Materials Needed:

For each student:
☐ None

For the leader:
☑ Chalkboard and chalk or chart paper and marker

Session Preparation:

Gather the necessary materials.

Session:

- Begin the group by asking one of the students to volunteer to be part of an experiment. Have that student leave the room.

- Draw two identical geometrical designs—straight lines, triangles, or rectangles—on the board/chart paper.

- Tell the group that it is their job to convince the student who is out of the room that one of the designs is longer or larger than the other one. They may do this through logical argument, bantering, or heckling. Emphasize that it is important that everyone participate by calling out comments rather than waiting to be called upon. Have the group agree which shape they will say is larger.

- Ask the student volunteer to come back into the room. Begin the commentary as soon as the student is asked, "Which (NAME OF SHAPE DRAWN) is larger?" Have the activity last from three to five minutes. (Watch the student volunteer carefully and stop the bantering if it is apparent that the student is being affected by the others. Do not subject the student to more pressure than necessary for him/her to experience a feeling of peer pressure.)

- Stop the commentary and tell the student what has taken place. Have the student describe how he/she felt about what just happened. Have the others tell how they felt when pressuring the student.

- Continue the lesson by having the students discuss peer pressure and how it affects decisions. Allow the students to share their personal experiences with peer pressure.

- Conclude the session by asking the students to be alert, between now and the next session, for examples of peer pressure in action.

EVERY DECISION HAS ALTERNATIVES AND OUTCOMES

Objective:

To have the students realize that every decision made involves alternatives and outcomes

Materials Needed:

For each student:
- ☑ Paper
- ☑ Pencil

For the leader:
- ☑ Chalkboard and chalk or chart paper and marker

Session Preparation:

On the board/chart paper, draw two diagrams as shown below:

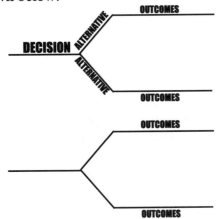

Gather any other necessary materials.

Session:

- Review the previous week's activity and give the students an opportunity to mention anything they have observed.

- Explain to the students that making a good decision is the way to counteract negative peer pressure. Using the diagram, review the basic decision-making skills. Do this by saying the students must first clarify the decision to be made (point to the word *Decision* on the diagram), then consider the alternatives (point to *Alternatives*), and finally consider each alternative's possible outcomes (point to *Outcomes*).

- Using the outline of the original diagram on the board/chart paper, give the following example:

  On the *Decision* line, write *Homework*.
  On one *Alternative* line, write *Do*.
  On the other *Alternative* line, write *Don't*.

  Ask the students to give examples of outcomes that may occur if someone does his/her homework and write those results in the space below *Outcomes*. Repeat the procedure for not doing homework. Write those examples above the word *Outcomes*.

- Ask the students to name other things they must make decisions about. Write their suggestions on the board/chart paper.

- Distribute paper and pencil to each student. Have the students draw a diagram. Then tell them to select one topic from the board/chart paper and complete the diagram in the same manner as the *Homework* diagram. Then have the students share their completed work.

- Conclude the session by reminding the students that every decision they make involves alternatives and outcomes and that they can make the best decision by thinking these things through before taking any action.

73

ACCEPTABLE AND UNACCEPTABLE RISKS

Objective:

To introduce the topic of *acceptable* and *unacceptable risks*

Materials Needed:

For each student:
- ☑ Paper
- ☑ Pencil

For the leader:
- ☑ Chalkboard and chalk or chart paper and marker

Session Preparation:

Gather the necessary materials.

Session:

- Distribute paper and a pencil to each student. Review the basics of decision making by having the students draw a diagram as they did in Session 2. Ask the students to name some decisions they must make that concern their peers. Write these on the board/chart paper. Have the students pick one decision and complete their diagram.

- Have the students share their completed diagrams.

- Ask the students what they feel is the most important ingredient in decision making. (The answer is *the outcome*.)

- Introduce the concept of *risk*. Discuss what constitutes an *acceptable risk*. (Acceptable risks provide opportunities to make new friends, have new and positive experiences, feel better about oneself, and increase personal resources. An acceptable risk is one that cannot harm people and things.) Introducing yourself to a new student would be an acceptable risk. Discuss what constitutes an *unacceptable risk*. (An unacceptable risk is one that can harm people and things.) Swimming in a river with a swift current would be an unacceptable risk.

- On the board/chart paper, make two columns. Label one *Acceptable Risks* and the other *Unacceptable Risks*. Have the students brainstorm about risks they think fit in either category. As they do this, write their suggestions in the proper columns. Then have the students evaluate what makes a risk acceptable or unacceptable.

- Conclude the session by asking the students to be alert for examples of *acceptable risks* or *unacceptable risks* that involve their peers. They should be prepared to discuss these risks at the next session.

CONSIDERING RISK FACTORS

Objective:

To help students understand that decisions should be made only after considering the risk factors associated with the outcomes

Materials Needed:

For each pair of students:
- ☑ Paper
- ☑ Pencil

For the leader:
- ☑ Paper
- ☑ Pencil

Session Preparation:

Gather the necessary materials.

Session:

- Have the students share any peer interactions they had or noticed and determine whether each interaction involved an *acceptable risk* or an *unacceptable risk.*

- Divide the students into pairs. Distribute paper and a pencil to each pair. Tell the students they have five minutes to write down as many situations as they can think of in which peers pressure others.

- When the allotted time has elapsed, tell the students that any decision they make, including those made because of peer pressure, must consider the risk factor associated with the outcome.

- Have the students share their answers. As each answer is shared, discuss what the risk factor would be; the outcomes; and, based on the outcome, whether it is an acceptable or unacceptable risk. Record the topic and the students' answers and save the paper for the next session.

- Conclude the session by asking each student to complete the following two sentences aloud:

    An acceptable risk I would take if asked by a peer would be ...

    An unacceptable risk I would not take if asked by a peer would be ...

GROUPS TO GO: SMALL GROUPS FOR COUNSELORS ON THE GO © 2006 MAR∗CO PRODUCTS, INC. 1-800-448-2197

EVALUATING ALTERNATIVES

Objective:

To help students become more aware of how decision making affects themselves and others

Materials Needed:

For each student:
    ☐ None

For the leader:
    ☑ Students' suggestion paper from Session 4

Session Preparation:

Gather the necessary materials.

Session:

• Introduce the session by having each student name a feeling. (An alternative would be to start with the letter "A" and have each student name a feeling that begins with a letter of the alphabet.)

• Review the topics and answers suggested in the last session, when the students named situations peers might ask them to be involved in. As each situation and decision is named, have the students answer the following questions:

How would I feel making this decision?

How would the person affected by the decision feel?

How did the decision affect others?

• Tell the students that people often do things they really do not want to do because they want to be accepted by a person or a group. Have the students answer the following question:

What would make a person give in to peer pressure in order to be accepted?

• Conclude the session by telling the students that peer pressure is not always bad. There are times that peers pressure you to do something that will benefit you. That is why, whenever peers want you to do something, it is important to evaluate the outcome and decide if you would be taking an acceptable or unacceptable risk.

SAYING "NO"

Objective:

To have the students role-play saying "No" in difficult situations involving peers

Materials Needed:

For each student:
□ None

For the leader:
□ None

Session Preparation:

None.

Session:

- Tell the students that it is easy to know, inside this room, what to do in a difficult situation involving peers. In this room, they are safe. That is not necessarily so outside. So today they are going to role-play saying "No" to a peer in a difficult situation.

- Present the following topics:

  Smoking cigarettes
  Shoplifting
  Lying to a parent
  Drinking alcohol
  Cheating on a test
  Telling another student's secret

- Divide the students into pairs and have each pair choose two topics. Have the students tell which two topics they want, making sure each topic is chosen at least once, preferably twice.

- Tell the students they have three minutes to work out the outline of their role-plays. In one role-play, one student is the peer and the other is the student being pressured. They should reverse roles for the second role-play. When the allotted time limit has elapsed, have the students present their role-plays. Call time after about two minutes and tell the students to switch to the second role-play. Call time after about two more minutes.

  (*Note:* If time allows, allow some students to perform their role-plays for the entire group.

- Conclude the group by asking each student to share one idea or fact that he/she felt was important or interesting during the group experience.

DIVORCE

The Feelings And Realities Of Divorce
Dealing With The Problems Of Divorce

THE FEELINGS AND REALITIES OF DIVORCE
(Grades 3-5)

Increasing numbers of children are dealing with divorce and its effect on their families. Schools are finding that these "children of divorce" need additional support and guidance in coping with the many problems that divorce adds to their lives.

The counselor can offer these children further support and coping skills in a small-group setting that gives the children the opportunity to relate to other children dealing with the same problems and time to discuss their feelings in a supportive and understanding atmosphere.

The six-session group *The Feelings And Realities Of Divorce* will focus on acknowledging that the divorce is real, that parents may look at the situation differently, how the divorce will affect them, adjustments to two households, and dealing with feelings.

When deciding which of the two divorce groups would be more appropriate for children in Grades 4 and 5, determine how mature the children are. Those with a high level of maturity would benefit more from *Dealing With The Problems Of Divorce*. This group could also be used with children who have participated already in *The Feelings And Realities Of Divorce* and who now need additional support.

This group is designed to help students:

- Realize that they are not alone
- Cope with their situation
- Discuss their feelings in a supportive and understanding atmosphere

Group candidates:

- Students whose parents are divorcing, have divorced, or are separated
- Six to eight students from the same or adjoining grade levels

Group preparation:

Interview each student selected individually and explain the purpose and process of the group. Then send a parent notification and permission letter (page 81).

Dear _____,

Divorce is a traumatic event for every family member. Unfortunately, the changes taking place in the family do not only affect the child when the child is at home. Feelings and fears regarding this family change stay with the child when the child is out of the home, whether at school or in other places.

Your child's classroom teacher has identified your child as a student who could benefit from extra help in understanding and coping with divorce.

In an effort to help your child and others learn more about divorce, I am forming a counseling group that will focus on helping children cope with their personal situations.

There will be six group meetings scheduled at a time the classroom teacher selects.

Your child knows about the group and has indicated that he or she would like to participate. However, no child is ever included in a small-group counseling program without his or her parents' knowledge and permission.

Please indicate, by completing the form below, that you wish to have your child participate in this group or that you do not want him or her to be included.

Return the permission slip to me by _____.

Thank you,

✂ -

☐ I, _____, *give permission* for my child to participate in the small-group counseling program for children of divorce.

☐ I, _____, *do not give permission* for my child to participate in the small-group counseling program for children of divorce.

Child's Name _____ Date _____

School _____ Grade _____

Teacher _____

Home Phone (____) _____ Work Phone (____) _____

Parent's Printed Name _____

Parent's Signature _____

DIVORCE IS REAL

Objective:

To help children get to know one another and learn to face the divorce without denying it, ignoring it, or pretending it isn't happening.

Materials Needed:

For each student:
☑ Drawing paper
☑ Crayons or markers

For the leader:
☑ Drawing paper
☑ Crayons or markers
☑ Chalkboard and chalk or chart paper and markers

Session Preparation:

Gather the necessary materials.

Session:

• Distribute drawing paper and crayons or markers to each child. Have the children print their names in large letters in the middle of their papers. Then have them write or draw something in each corner that tells something about them.

• As the children are completing their drawings, the leader should make a similar drawing. When the drawings are completed, the leader should share his/her drawing first, then have the children share theirs.

• Prepare the children for the group by telling them that each of them is experiencing divorce and this group will be talking about what divorce is like and looking for the best ways for each of them to handle their situation.

• Explain that the students will be talking about very personal things that they may not want shared anywhere but in this group. So it is important that no one talk outside this room about what anyone says in the group. Each group member may talk about what he/she says with his/her family members.

• Be very frank when telling the children that one of the first things children of divorce (or COD's as they are often called) must do is face the facts. They cannot ignore the divorce. They must admit that their parents are divorcing or have already divorced.

• Have those children who are willing to do so answer the following questions:

How did you find out about your parents' divorce?

When you found out, how did you feel? (As the children express their feelings, write them on the board/chart paper. Each time the same feeling is mentioned, put a checkmark behind the word that describes it.)

• Review the feelings listed, pointing out similarities and differences.

• Conclude the session by reviewing the purpose of the group. Ask the children if they have any concerns or questions. Then remind them when and where the next meeting will take place. Have the children take their pictures home.

EVERYONE DOES NOT SEE DIVORCE IN THE SAME WAY

Objective:

To help children accept their parents' divorce and realize that each of their parents may look at the situation differently

Materials Needed:

For each student:
☑ Copy of *How Divorce Works* (page 84)
☑ Pencil

For the leader:
☐ None

Session Preparation:

Reproduce *How Divorce Works* for each student. Gather any other necessary materials.

Session:

• Begin the session by asking if anyone wants to share any thoughts, feelings, or experiences about his/her parents' divorce. (Pause for responses.)

• Tell the students that in this session, they will be talking about how divorce works.

• Distribute *How Divorce Works* and a pencil to each child. Have the children complete the activity sheet by writing what they believe each person would say about how divorce works.

• Have the children share their responses. Using the various answers, summarize for the group the various ways divorce works.

• Conclude the session by telling the children that the sooner they accept the divorce and talk about it, the sooner they will start to feel better about their lives and situations. Denying or pretending the divorce isn't happening will only make things harder.

• Tell the children when and where the next session will take place. Have them take their papers home and encourage them to share them with their parent(s).

HOW DIVORCE WORKS

Directions: Imagine that you are wondering about divorce. You are not sure how it works or what is going to happen. Then imagine you ask both your mother and father, "How does divorce work?" Write on the lines provided what you think they would say. Then write what *you* think about how divorce works.

My mother says _____

_____

_____

_____ .

My father says _____

_____

_____

_____ .

I think _____

_____

_____

_____ .

DIVORCE WILL CHANGE EVERYONE'S LIFE

Objective:

To help children explore what is actually going to happen as a result of the divorce and how it will affect or is already affecting them

Materials Needed:

For each student:
- ☑ Paper
- ☑ Pencil
- ☑ Art paper
- ☑ Crayons or markers

For the leader:
- ☐ None

Session Preparation:

Gather the necessary materials.

Session:

- Begin the session by asking if any of the children want to share any thoughts, feelings, or experiences regarding his/her divorce situation.

- Distribute paper and a pencil to each child. Have the children write the answers to the following questions on the paper.

  (*Note:* If the children are unsure of the answer to any of these questions, suggest they discuss the questions with each of their parents. If their mothers' answers from are different from their fathers' answers, suggest that the children speak with you privately to help them make sense of what is going on and why they are getting different answers.)

- Read each question aloud, pausing to allow the children time to write their responses.

  When will or did your parents' divorce go into effect or when was it final?

  After the divorce is final, who will have custody of you or who has custody of you now?

  Who will you live with after the divorce? Who do you live with now?

  Where will you live after the divorce? Where do you live with now?

  When will you see the parent you don't live with? When do you see that parent now?

- After the children have answered the questions, ask:

  How do you feel about your answers?

  How do you think these answers will affect your life?

- Distribute a piece of art paper and crayons or markers to each child. Have the children draw a picture of how they feel divorce has changed their lives. Have the children share their completed drawings with the group.

- Conclude the session by telling the children that their parents' divorce will change some parts of their lives. Some changes will be good and some may not be so good, but the children need to know they can learn to adjust to every change.

- Remind the children when and where the next session will take place. Have them take their papers home and encourage them to share them with their parent(s).

DIVORCE CAUSES MANY FEELINGS

Objective:

To help children face their feelings about their parents' divorce and handle themselves appropriately

Materials Needed:

For each student:
☐ None

For the leader:
☑ 9 index cards
☑ Chart paper and marker

Session Preparation:

Write one of the following words on each index card: *lonely, confused, guilty, insecure, rejected, embarrassed, cheated, angry, powerless*. Gather any other necessary materials.

Session:

- Begin the session by asking if anyone wants to share any thoughts, feelings, or experiences regarding his/her divorce situation.

- Hold the cards so the words cannot be seen and have each child select a card. Then have the children read the word on their cards aloud and think of a situation related to their parents' divorce that made them feel like the word on the card. They should not say anything at this time.

   (*Note:* For younger children, read the words aloud. If any of the children are not sure of a word's meaning, explain the meaning to the child.)

- Divide the group into partners. Have one partner tell the other partner the situation he/she thought of. The listener should try to guess the feeling word that the situation was portraying. If, after several attempts, the listener is unable to guess the word, the word should be revealed. Then the partners should reverse the roles.

- When the partners have finished, have the group as a whole talk about the words on the cards. As each word is presented, list these words on the chart paper. Save this list for the next session.

- Conclude the session by telling the children that they will have many similar and many different feelings about their parents' divorces. Assure them that each feeling is OK and that in the next session you will talk more about these feelings.

IDENTIFYING PERSONAL SITUATIONS THAT INVOKE CERTAIN FEELINGS

Objective:

To help children more fully understand their feelings about their parents' divorce and talk about ways to cope with these feelings

Materials Needed:

For each student:
☐ None

For the leader:
☑ List of words from Session 4
☑ Marker

Session Preparation:

Gather the necessary materials.

Session:

• Begin the session by asking if anyone wants to share any thoughts, feelings, or experiences regarding his/her divorce situation.

• Using the list from the previous session, present the words one by one. After each word is presented, give the explanation which follows it and ask the question following it. Allow time after each question for the children to comment, give personal examples, or ask questions of each other or the leader.

    Lonely—If you have felt lonely since your parents' divorce, remember that it takes two people to create a relationship and you must do your part to make the relationship go well. What could you do with your mother and father that would help both of you feel less lonely?

    Confused—If you feel confused when your parents argue, try not to be around when they do. Stay out of their arguments and don't take sides with either parent. Where could you go when your parents argue?

    Guilty—If your parents' divorce makes you feel guilty, realize that you did not make your parents decide to divorce. Do you ever feel guilty?

    Insecure—If you feel insecure because of your parents' divorce, you need to remember that at least one parent will be there to take care of you and protect you. Which parent do you think that will be?

    Rejected—If your parents' divorce causes you to feel rejected, remember that although your parents are no longer married to each other they are not rejecting you. What has happened to make you feel rejected?

    Embarrassed—If your parents' divorce embarrasses you, you need to realize that there are many children whose parents are divorced. How many children do you know whose parents are divorced?

    Cheated—If you feel cheated because of your parents' divorce, remember no situation is perfect. Try to find the good things about your situation and think about them. What are some good things about your situation?

Angry—If you feel angry because of your parents' divorce, you should talk with your parents or other adults about your anger and how to deal with it. Who could you talk with about your anger?

Powerless—If you feel powerless because of your parents' divorce, remember that even though you have no control over what happens between your mother and father, you have control over what happens between you and your parents. What is one situation with either your mother or father that you can control to some extent?

• Conclude the session by asking the children if they can think of any other feelings they have had about their parents divorce.

• Add any additional feelings mentioned to the list. When the list is completed, read each word and ask the children to raise their hands if they have ever felt this way. Tally the number of raised hands and write that number after the word.

• Conclude the lesson by telling the children that whenever they have any of the feelings on the chart, they are to remember that they are not alone with these feelings. Others in the group and children of divorce who are not in the group also have these feelings.

• Inform the children that the next session will be the last session.

GROUPS TO GO: SMALL GROUPS FOR COUNSELORS ON THE GO © 2006 MAR*CO PRODUCTS, INC. 1-800-448-2197

MAKING THE BEST OF A NEW SITUATION

Objective:

To help children think of things they can do that will help them feel better about their new situation and learn to adjust to it.

Materials Needed:

For each student:
- ☑ Paper
- ☑ Pencil

For the leader:
- ☐ None

Session Preparation:

Gather the necessary materials.

Session:

- Begin the session by asking the children to name two things they enjoy doing. (Pause for responses.)

- Then tell them that doing things they like to do will help them feel better and not think so much about their family's situation. When they begin to feel some of the ways discussed in the last two sessions, they can help themselves feel better by doing something they enjoy.

- Distribute paper and a pencil to each child and ask the children to list things they did not like about living with their parents when they were married.

- Have the children share their answers with the group.

- Tell the children to keep this list where they can find it easily. Then when they start to wish things were like they used to be, they should read their list and be glad they don't have to deal with these things any more.

- Have the children turn their papers over and list all the things they like about their new situation.

- Have the children share their answers with the group.

- Tell the children that when they begin to feel upset with their new situation, they should take out their list, read it, and feel grateful for the good things in their new situation.

- Have each child complete the following statements aloud:

  Divorce is …

  From this group, I learned …

- Conclude the group by telling the children that although this is their last session together, it is important that they continue to talk about their thoughts and feelings about their parents' divorce. Remind them that it takes a long time to adjust to a new situation.

- Thank the children for their participation. Tell them that you are always available to meet with them if they need to talk with someone. Have them take their papers home.

DEALING WITH THE PROBLEMS OF DIVORCE
(Grades 4-5)

Children often feel caught between parents who are separated, divorced, or divorcing. Confusion, anger, and fear overtake children's lives as they try to decipher how to react to situations without hurting either their mother or father.

The five-session group *Dealing With The Problems Of Divorce* will focus on helping children develop plans of action to cope with the hurts of divorce, being "caught in the middle," and other concerns children need to discuss with their parents when a divorce is taking or has taken place.

This group is designed to help students:

- Discuss their concerns with their parents
- Make a plan to handle delicate situations that will satisfy everyone involved

Group candidates:

- Students whose parents are divorcing, have divorced, or are separated
- Students whose parents may be involving them in divorce problems
- Six to eight students from the same or adjoining grade levels

Group preparation:

Interview each student selected individually and explain the purpose and process of the group. Then send a parent notification and permission letter (page 91).

Dear _____,

Divorce is a traumatic event for every family member. Children are often confused, angry, and fearful about what is happening and uncertain how to handle delicate situations. Unfortunately these feelings do not only affect the child when the child is at home. The feelings and fears regarding this family change stay with the child when the child is out of the home, whether at school or in other places.

Your child's classroom teacher has identified your child as a student who could benefit from extra help in understanding and coping with divorce.

In an effort to help your child and others learn more about divorce, I am forming a counseling group that will focus on helping children cope with their personal situations.

There will be five group meetings scheduled at a time the classroom teacher selects.

Your child knows about the group and has indicated that he or she would like to participate. However, no child is ever included in a small-group counseling program without his or her parents' knowledge and permission.

Please indicate, by completing the form below, that you wish to have your child participate in this group or that you do not want him or her to be included.

Return the permission slip to me by _____.

Thank you,

✂- -

☐ I, _____, *give permission* for my child to participate in the small-group counseling program for children of divorce.

☐ I, _____, *do not give permission* for my child to
participate in the small-group counseling program for children of divorce.

Child's Name _____ Date _____

School _____ Grade _____

Teacher _____

Home Phone (_____) _____ Work Phone (_____) _____

Parent's Printed Name _____

Parent's Signature _____

91

SIGNS OF A SHAKY PARENTAL RELATIONSHIP

Objective:

To discuss the confusion that often occurs in a household before the children are told that their parents are separating

Materials Needed:

For each student:
  ☐ None

For the leader:
  ☑ Index cards
  ☑ Marker

Session Preparation:

Using the marker, write on each index card an example of a change a child may see but not understand. Examples would be: parents fighting, one parent not home as much any more, parents losing their tempers with children, money problems, emotional outbursts such as crying or yelling, depression, etc.

Session:

• Distribute an index card to each child. Have each child read his/her card aloud. Then ask the children:

  Are any of these situations familiar to you?

  When you saw these situations in your home, did you think they would lead to a divorce?

  Have you discussed any of these situations with your parents?

  Have your parents discussed any of these situations with you?

• Explain that children are often unaware that their parents are having problems. Then ask:

  Were any of you aware that your parents were having problems?

• Continuing to use the statements on the index cards, ask the children to whom the situations were familiar the following question:

  When you were noticing the situations, why did you think your parents were behaving that way? (**Note:** Many, if not all, children will give reasons that sound like excuses for their parents' behavior.)

• Continue by telling the children that when they see changes in their parents' behavior, it is normal to find excuses rather than admit that their parents are having difficulty. Then ask:

  Why do you think children do not want to admit that their parents are having difficulties?

• Conclude the session by asking the children to think about what was happening in their households and name one or more "clues" they may not have noticed at the time that signaled that their parents' relationship was in trouble.

Objective:

To have the children verbalize their feelings about being "in the middle" and learn ways to avoid being in that situation

Materials Needed:

For each student:
- ☑ Copy of *Plan Of Action I* (page 95)
- ☑ Pencil

For the leader:
- ☑ Chalkboard and chalk or chart paper and marker

Session Preparation:

Reproduce *Plan Of Action I* for each child. Gather any other necessary materials.

Session:

- Begin the session by asking the children to name situations in which someone is "in the middle." Write the children's answers on the board/chart paper. If being "in the middle" of divorced parents is not mentioned, add it to the list.

- Tell the children that being "in the middle" is not always an uncomfortable situation and that if it isn't, there is no problem. But for today, the group is going to think about times when "being in the middle" situations are uncomfortable. Give the following example:

Betty is friends with Sue and Cindy. She likes both of them, but they do not like each other. Betty feels as if she is constantly negotiating to stay friends with both because they each get upset if she does something with or says something nice about the other.

- Ask the children if this has ever happened to them or if they know of someone to whom it has happened. (*Note:* As the children develop this topic, they will most likely mention being "in the middle" between divorced parents.)

- Let the children know that children often feel as if they are "in the middle" between divorced parents. Explain that this happens when parents make statements like:

  When you see your father, tell him he forgot to send his support check last week.

  Tell your mother to send you some decent clothes to wear when you visit.

- Explain that children want to please both parents, but their parents are putting them in situations that make them uncomfortable. Then ask:

  What is it like—or what do you think it would be like—to be in an "in the middle" situation between divorced parents?

- Once children have admitted that they often feel "in the middle" when parents are divorcing, ask what they have done when they are in an "in the middle" situation and how well it worked. Record their suggestions on the board/chart paper.

- When all the suggestions have been listed, review those that were successful, circling them on the board/chart paper.

- Distribute *Plan Of Action I* and a pencil to each child. Explain that for the duration of the group, they will be making *Plans Of Action* for several topics and that this is the first of these. Then tell the children to think about what was discussed in the group and write their personal *Plan Of Action I* about being "in the middle."

- Have the each child share his/her completed *Plan Of Action I.*

- Conclude the session by asking the children who are in this situation to discuss their *Plan Of Action I* with their parents.

94

PLAN OF ACTION I

Dear Mom and Dad,

When you ask me to _____

_____

_____

_____,

I feel like I am "in the middle."

This is very hard for me. From now on, when I feel like you are putting me "in the middle," I am going to _____

_____

_____

_____

_____

_____.

Your child,

_____

GROUPS TO GO: SMALL GROUPS FOR COUNSELORS ON THE GO © 2006 MAR•CO PRODUCTS, INC. 1-800-448-2197

NOT TALKING ABOUT ONE PARENT WITH THE OTHER

Objective:

To discuss the problem of talking about one parent with another

Materials Needed:

For each student:
- ☑ Copy of *Plan Of Action II* (page 97)
- ☑ Pencil

For the leader:
- ☑ Chalkboard and chalk or chart paper and marker

Session Preparation:

Reproduce *Plan Of Action II* for each child. Gather any other necessary materials.

Session:

- Review the *Plans Of Action I* from Session 2 and encourage the children to give feedback about how their individual plans succeeded or failed.

- Tell the children that many children feel uneasy talking about one parent with the other. Then ask:

    Can you name some reasons this statement is true?

- Record the children's answers on a board/chart paper. Then discuss, in depth, each reason given by the children. Direct the discussion so the children will better understand why their parents are naturally curious about each other, the bitterness their parents may be harboring toward each other, and their parents' feelings toward each other. *(Note:* This is important. Too often children see only their side of the situation and do not realize the emotional trauma their parents are experiencing.)

- Have the children role-play talking with their parents about why they don't want to talk about one parent with another. Be sure every child role-plays both the child and the parent.

- Distribute *Plan Of Action II* and a pencil to each child. Then tell the children to remember what has been discussed and write a second *Plan Of Action* that will tell how they plan to *not* talk about one parent with the other.

- Have the children share their completed *Plans Of Action II* with the group.

- Conclude the session by asking the children to discuss their *Plan Of Action II* with their parents.

PLAN OF ACTION II

Dear Mom and Dad,

There are times when I need to talk with one of you about the other. When I would like to do this, I feel _____

_____

_____ .

This is not a feeling I like. From now on when a situation arises and I need to talk about one of you to the other, I am going to _____

_____

_____

_____

_____ .

Your child,

_____

GROUPS TO GO: SMALL GROUPS FOR COUNSELORS ON THE GO © 2006 MAR★CO PRODUCTS, INC. 1-800-448-2197

LIVING IN TWO DIFFERENT HOUSEHOLDS

Objective:

To discuss the adjustments that must be made when living in two different households

Materials Needed:

For each student:
- ☑ Copy of *Plan Of Action III* (page 100)
- ☑ Pencil
- ☑ Paper

For the leader:
- ☑ Chalkboard and chalk or chart paper and marker

Session Preparation:

Reproduce *Plan Of Action III* for each child. Gather any other necessary materials.

Session:

- Begin the session by reviewing the *Plans Of Action II* from Session 3. Have the children report on how their plans worked.

- Tell the children that it is often difficult and confusing for children whose parents are divorced to follow the rules set down in the two different households in which they live.

- Distribute paper and pencils to the children. Tell them to list as many rules as they can think of in three minutes. The rules may be those of either parent or both parents.

- Tell the children to begin. Time the exercise. When he allotted time has elapsed, have the children look at their lists and identify each rule by putting an "M" after a rule that exists only in their mother's household, an "F" after a rule that exists only in their father's household, and a "B" after a rule that exists in both households.

- Select one child to read his/her list and tell how he/she coded each rule. As the list is being read, have the other children mark off every identical rule on their lists. Then have another child read only the rules on his/her list that are not marked off because the first child's list included them. Again, have the other children mark off every identical rule on their lists. Continue until all the children have had a turn to read their lists. (*Note:* If a child's list is completely marked off before his/her turn, tell him/her to say so, then call on the next child.)

- On the board/chart paper, tally up the number of identical rules and the number that are different. Then ask the children why they think parents seem to have similar rules.

- Tell the children to select, from their list, one rule that exists in one household and not in the other. Encourage the students to select the rule that they have the most difficulty dealing with. Have them tell the group what rule they chose.

- When the last rule has been read, present the following questions. Initiate a discussion about each question.

    Why is having different household rules normal?

Is it difficult to accept both parents' rules?

What are some ways to adjust to living in two different households?

- Distribute *Plan Of Action III* to each child. Tell the children to remember what the group discussed as they complete their activity sheets. Have them share what they have written with the group.

- Conclude the session by asking the children to discuss their *Plan Of Action III* with their parents.

PLAN OF ACTION III

Dear Mom and Dad,

Each of you has rules that you expect me to follow. Some of your rules are the same. Others are not. Mom, the rule that is the most difficult for me to follow at your house is _____

_____.

Dad, the rule that is the most difficult for me to follow at your house is _____

_____.

I know it is important for me to follow these rules, so I have come up with the following plans that are positive and will cause the least amount of conflict.

Mom, at your house, I am going to _____

_____

_____.

Dad, at your house, I am going to _____

_____

_____.

Your child,

_____

GROUPS TO GO: SMALL GROUPS FOR COUNSELORS ON THE GO © 2006 MAR*CO PRODUCTS, INC. 1-800-448-2197

DIVORCE CAUSES HURT

Objective:

To help students understand everyone touched by a divorce situation experiences hurts, but that the ultimate goal is for everyone to continue on with their lives in the most productive way possible

Materials Needed:

For each student:
- ☑ Copy of *Plan Of Action IV* (page 102)
- ☑ Pencil
- ☑ Paper

For the leader:
- ☐ None

Session Preparation:

Reproduce *Plan Of Action IV* for each child. Gather any other necessary materials.

Session:

- Begin the session by reviewing the *Plans Of Action III* from Session 4. Have the children report on how their plans worked.

- Tell the children that divorce is a painful situation and that every painful situation hurts.

- Distribute paper and pencils to the children. Tell them to list as many ways as they can think of that their parents' divorce hurt them.

- Divide the children into pairs. Tell them to discuss each item on their list with their partner and describe how they coped with the hurt. (***Note:*** A child who has not been able to cope with a specific hurt should only identify the hurt. At this time, the child should not discuss how he/she tried to cope with the hurt.)

- When everyone has finished the activity, ask the children the following question. Lead the discussion to encourage the children to mention the "will to survive."

    Why do you believe people learn to cope with painful or difficult situations?

- Tell the children that most people want to survive and, in order to do so, must learn to cope with their hurts. Emphasize that persevering toward this goal will help them lead a more productive and satisfying life.

- Instruct the children that they may now tell their partners about any hurt they have not been able to cope with. Tell the partners to give suggestions they believe will help the other student to cope. Then have the children share the suggestions made to them.

- Distribute *Plan Of Action IV* to each child and have each child form a plan to overcome hurt. If time allows, have the children share their completed plans before taking them home to share with their parents.

- Conclude the group by thanking the children for their participation. Remind them that you are available and willing to listen if they ever need to discuss anything with you. Congratulate them on the way they discussed the different subjects, and tell them they can overcome the unhappiness of their families' situations and lead productive lives.

GROUPS TO GO: SMALL GROUPS FOR COUNSELORS ON THE GO © 2006 MAR*CO PRODUCTS, INC. 1-800-448-2197

PLAN OF ACTION IV

Dear Mom and Dad,

I have learned that divorce hurts everyone.
Some of the hurts I have felt are:

_____

_____

_____

_____ .

I have also learned that in order to lead a more productive
and satisfying life, I need to overcome the hurts.

My plan to cope with my hurts is: _____

_____

_____

_____

_____ .

Your child,

_____

GROUPS TO GO: SMALL GROUPS FOR COUNSELORS ON THE GO © 2006 MAR✱CO PRODUCTS, INC. 1-800-448-2197

GRIEF AND LOSS

Coping With Death

Somewhere Over The Rainbow

COPING WITH DEATH
(Grades 3-5)

Death may be unexpected, as in the case of an automobile accident or it may be anticipated as a result of a long illness. In either case, the counselor must be prepared to actively assist the child experiencing the loss. Because death is usually a singular event affecting one child or one family, counselors usually deal with children individually rather than with groups. However, multiple deaths do occur. In these situations, the counselor may want to approach the children through a group-counseling experience.

It is important for counselors to realize that young children have particular needs in regard to death education or counseling. Although these children realize that death is final, they may not internalize the fact that it will happen to everyone, including themselves. Children this age are influenced by what peers say about death as well as by what they learn from adults and the media. They are also prone to develop fears and become anxious when they face a death associated with violence. It is important that counselors working with children who have experienced a death allow them to discuss their feelings openly and honestly.

Coping With Death centers around discussion and is especially appropriate for children who can communicate with others. The second group, *Somewhere Over The Rainbow,* is more structured and more appropriate for children who may need more visual aids in order to express their feelings.

This group is designed to help students:

- Understand the reality of death and that anyone can die any time
- Cope with their personal situations
- Discuss their feelings in a supportive and understanding atmosphere

Group candidates:

- Children who have experienced the death of a parent, relative, sibling, friend, or even a pet
- Four to six students from the same or adjoining grade levels

Group preparation:

Interview each student selected individually and explain the purpose and process of the group. Then send a parent notification and permission letter (page 105).

Dear _____,

Death is a traumatic event for every family member. Feelings expressed and not expressed do not go away when the child leaves the house. They are always present and may pop up and become primary at any time during the school day. When this happens, children cannot focus on the tasks being presented in the classroom.

Your child's classroom teacher has identified your child as a student who could benefit from extra help in understanding and coping with a death.

In an effort to help your child and others learn more about this topic, I am forming a counseling group that will focus on helping children cope with deaths that have affected them.

There will be six group meetings scheduled at a time the classroom teacher selects.

Your child knows about the group and has indicated that he or she would like to participate. However, no child is ever included in a small-group counseling program without his or her parents' knowledge and permission.

Please indicate, by completing the form below, that you wish to have your child participate in this group or that you do not want him or her to be included.

Return the permission slip to me by _____.

Thank you,

✂ -

☐ I, _____, *give permission* for my child to partici-
pate in the small-group counseling program for children experiencing difficulty in dealing with the death of a loved one.

☐ I, _____, *do not give permission* for my child to
participate in the small-group counseling program for children experiencing difficulty in dealing with the death of a loved one.

Child's Name _____   Date _____

School _____   Grade _____

Teacher _____

Home Phone (____) _____   Work Phone (____) _____

Parent's Printed Name _____

Parent's Signature _____

COPING WITH DEATH—WHAT IS DEATH?

Objective:

To understand each child's conception of death

Materials Needed:

For each child:
- ☑ Different colors of construction paper
- ☑ Crayons or markers

For the leader:
- ☑ Group folder or a folder for each individual group member

Session Preparation:

Gather the necessary materials.

Session:

- Stack different-colored construction paper and crayons or markers in a central location.

- Explain to the children that they will be meeting as a group for six sessions because everyone in the group has experienced the death of someone important to him/her.

- Ask each child to repeat and complete the following sentence:

  My name is _____ and the person I lost who was important to me was (NAME THE PERSON LOST).

- Tell the children that the word *death* means something to everyone, and it does not have to mean the same thing to each person. Then say:

  I would like each of you to draw a picture of death. *Select a piece of construction paper and crayons (markers). Then draw what you think of when you hear the word* death.

  (***Note:*** Some children may draw pictures of common symbols of death such as a skeleton, an angel, a ghost, a cemetery, a casket, or a funeral procession. Others may just color their paper to show something like darkness.)

- Have the children share their pictures. Then discuss the likenesses and differences between the children's perceptions of death and the realities of death. (***Note:*** Children of this age are most likely to be very curious about death. This curiosity will help them deal with the reality of death.)

- Collect the pictures. Keep them in either a group folder or in each group member's individual folder.

GROUPS TO GO: SMALL GROUPS FOR COUNSELORS ON THE GO © 2006 MAR*CO PRODUCTS, INC. 1-800-448-2197

IT DIDN'T REALLY HAPPEN

Objective:

To help the children understand the importance of expressing their feelings about the death rather than bottling them up

Materials Needed:

For each child:
☐ None

For the leader:
☐ None

Session Preparation:

None.

Session:

(*Note:* In the initial stages of loss, children experience shock and denial just as adults do. Adults are often puzzled because children do not cry, refuse to talk about the person who has died, or refuse to discuss the death itself. Since adults usually do not react in this manner, the child's behavior is confusing.)

• Begin the session by saying:

Tell us about the different ways people feel when they lose someone important to them. (Crying will be mentioned, and it is important to explain that crying is a good way to release emotion.)

• Then ask:

Why do you think people cry when they lose someone important to them? (Accept all appropriate answers.)

How do people usually feel after they have cried? (relieved, better, etc.) *Why is this so?* (When you lose someone important to you, you feel many different emotions. Crying is one way to let those emotions out.)

If a person doesn't cry, does that mean he or she doesn't care as much as the person who does cry? (No.)

What are some other ways a person might let his or her emotions out? (People might feel anger, jealousy, withdrawal, and any other appropriate answer.)

• Use the remainder of the session to allow each child to talk about the person who has died and about that person's importance in the child's life.

Session 3
FEAR

Objective:

To discuss the fears the children have experienced since the death

Materials Needed:

For each child:
☐ None

For the leader:
☑ Chalkboard and chalk or chart paper and marker

Session Preparation:

Gather the necessary materials.

Session:

(*Note:* Children who have lost a parent often fear losing the remaining parent. If a sibling has died, children are often fearful that they, too, may die. In this session, it is important to openly discuss these fears.)

- Begin the session by reading aloud the following scenario:

  Jerry and his uncle are visiting the zoo. All of a sudden, there is a terrible commotion. People are screaming and zoo attendants are running. Then Jerry and his uncle see the problem. A lion is loose and running toward them.

  Would most people be afraid in this situation?

  Would you be afraid?

- Continue the session by reading aloud the following scenarios:

  You're riding in your family's car, sitting in the back seat, playing a videogame. Your mother screams and your dad slams on the brakes. The car swerves toward the edge of the road. It takes only a second for you to realize that you're going to be hit by a large truck that is coming right toward you.

  Would most people be afraid in this situation?

  Would you be afraid?

  The weather is horrible. The wind is blowing, and it is raining harder than you have ever seen. The sky is dark, and so is your house, because the electricity is off. A warning you hear over your battery-operated radio tells you not to leave your house, because hurricane-force winds will be over your area in less than 20 minutes.

  Would most people be afraid in this situation?

  Would you be afraid?

- Continue by asking the children why most people would be afraid in situations like these. (They would be afraid because they might get hurt or even die. All of a sudden, they are in a life-threatening situation over which they have no control.)

- Tell the children that it is normal to be afraid in dangerous situations. Then ask the children to name other situations that might make them fearful. If death isn't named, ask the following questions:

108

What about death? Can the death of some-one important to you make you fearful? Why? (Death makes you fearful because you might wonder if you are going to die, too.)

- Continue by assuring the children that it is normal to feel fearful after the death of an important person. Then ask:

  What kinds of fears did you experience?

- Write their contributions on the board/chart paper and discuss each one in detail. Since this is the most important part of the session, give the children ample time to discuss their concerns.

- Conclude the lesson by reassuring the children that fear is normal and something that everyone experiences.

Objective:

To help the children realize that angry feelings over a death are normal

Materials Needed:

For each child:
  ☑ Copy of *Things That Make Me Angry* (page 111)
  ☑ Pencil

For the leader:
  ☑ Individual folders or group folder

Session Preparation:

Reproduce *Things That Make Me Angry* for each child. Gather any other necessary materials.

Session:

- Begin the session by telling the children that in this session, they will be learning about another normal emotion that occurs when someone dies. That emotion is *anger*. Like fear, anger is normal. Everyone experiences angry feelings when he/she loses someone he/she loves.

- Have each child name one thing that has made him/her angry since the death.

- Distribute *Things That Make Me Angry* and a pencil to each child. Tell the children to list all the things they are angry about because their important person died.

- When the children have completed their lists, tell them to put a 1 next to the thing that makes them most angry, and continue until they get to the last thing on their list.

- Spend the remainder of the time going over each item on their lists and discussing ways of dealing with the anger. For example:

  A child who has lost a mother may be angry about having more responsibilities at home. Discuss why it may be necessary for the child to do more at home and how he/she can do everything that must be accomplished. If poor organization makes the child's responsibilities seem overwhelming, help set up a schedule. If the child's responsibilities are overwhelming because his/her father has too many expectations, suggest a way to communicate with that parent.

- Collect the children's activity sheets and place them in the individual folders or group folder.

- Conclude the session by telling the children that although their anger is normal, it is not okay to take their anger out on other people or on property.

Name_____   Date_____

THINGS THAT MAKE ME ANGRY

I was very sad when _____ died.

I didn't want it to happen.

Because of _____'s death,
it makes me angry that I will no longer be able to:

_____

_____

_____

_____

_____ .

Because of _____'s death,
it makes me angry that I now have to:

_____

_____

_____

_____

_____ .

Objective:

To explore the feelings of guilt associated with death and help the children understand that guilt feelings are normal, but that there is no reason for them to feel guilty

Materials Needed:

For each child:
- ☐ None

For the leader:
- ☐ None

Session Preparation:

None.

Session:

- Ask the children the meaning of the word *guilt*. Discuss that *guilt* is a feeling people have when they regret doing something or feel they are to blame for something. Then have the children name some things people often feel guilty about (telling a lie, stealing, cheating on a test, etc.). Make it clear that feeling guilt because of a regret is a normal feeling, just as *anger* and *fear* are normal feelings.

- Ask the children if they have ever heard someone wish that he/she had done something differently for, with, or to a person who had died.

- Explain that it is normal to wish you had done something different for a special person in your life who has died. There will always be regrets, no matter when a person dies.

- Ask the children the following questions:

  What regrets might a person have if a special person dies at a very young age? (A person might feel he/she should have played with the person more, been kinder to the person, etc.)

  What regrets might a person have if a special person dies at a very old age? (A person might regret that he/she didn't visit the elderly person more, spend more time with him/her, didn't listen to him/her more, etc.)

  What regrets might a person have if a special person dies after a long illness? (A person might regret not spending more time with him/her, not having more patience, not doing some extra things to make the person more comfortable, etc.)

- Ask the children to think about their special person who has died. Have them think whether there is something they regret not doing. As each child names his/her regrets, ask the following questions:

  Why do you feel guilty for not doing this?

  What do you wish you had done instead?

  Do you think the person you lost would understand why you did not do what you're feeling guilty about?

  Do you think the person you lost would want you to feel guilty?

- Conclude the lesson by telling the children that regrets and guilt will always be a part of death, but that the person they lost would understand why these things happened, loved them very much, and would not want them to feel guilty.

Session 6
REMEMBERING

(*Note:* It is important that children remember the person who has died as realistically as possible. Have the children discuss the good qualities of the person who has died as well as his/her less desirable qualities. Discussing both types of qualities gives the children a realistic memory of the person, rather than an idealized memory. Idealization of a person who has died often leaves the child with an unrealistic memory that could affect his/her development. For example, if a sibling who dies is idealized as perfect, the child might feel unable to live up to the reputation of the child who died. Emphasize the importance of remembering, but remembering reality.)

Objective:

To encourage each child to remember his/her special person as realistically as possible

Materials Needed:

For each child:
  ☐ None

For the leader:
  ☑ Children's folders with activity sheets or activity sheets without folders

Session Preparation:

Gather the necessary materials.

Session:

• Tell the children that they will spend this final session remembering the special person each of them has lost.

• Select one group member. Guide him/her through the process of remembering by saying:

> *Take one minute to talk about your special person.* (Time the child for exactly one minute. When one minute has elapsed, continue.)

> *What good things can you tell us about your special person?*

> *What things about your special person were not so good?*

Continue with the process until each child has had an opportunity to participate.

• Return the pictures drawn in the first session. Ask the children:

> *Do you remember what this drawing was about?* (It was a drawing of the perception of *death*.)

> *If you were drawing this picture today, would it be the same or would you change it? Why?*

• If you are using individual folders, distribute them to the students with the anger worksheet completed in Session 4. Tell the children they may take their folder, worksheet, and drawing home.

• Conclude the session by thanking the children for their participation. Emphasize the importance of remembering, but remind them that memories must be real.

113

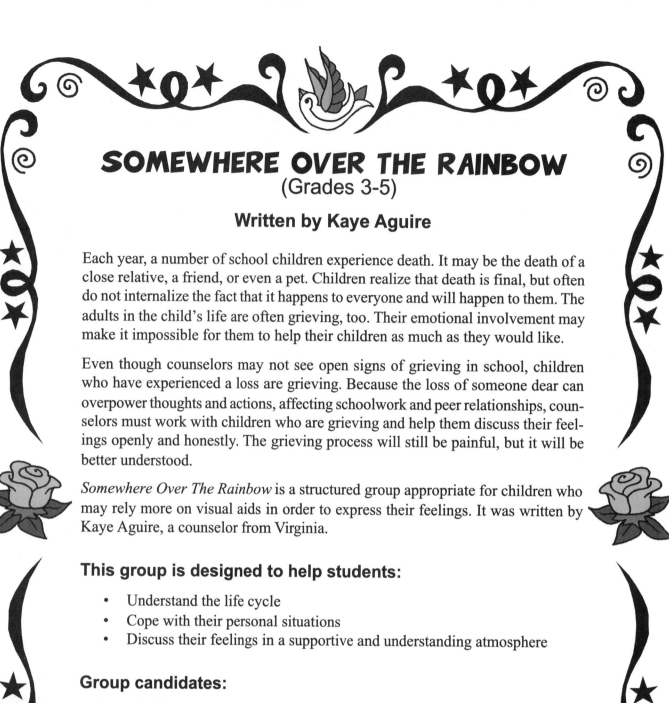

SOMEWHERE OVER THE RAINBOW
(Grades 3-5)

Written by Kaye Aguire

Each year, a number of school children experience death. It may be the death of a close relative, a friend, or even a pet. Children realize that death is final, but often do not internalize the fact that it happens to everyone and will happen to them. The adults in the child's life are often grieving, too. Their emotional involvement may make it impossible for them to help their children as much as they would like.

Even though counselors may not see open signs of grieving in school, children who have experienced a loss are grieving. Because the loss of someone dear can overpower thoughts and actions, affecting schoolwork and peer relationships, counselors must work with children who are grieving and help them discuss their feelings openly and honestly. The grieving process will still be painful, but it will be better understood.

Somewhere Over The Rainbow is a structured group appropriate for children who may rely more on visual aids in order to express their feelings. It was written by Kaye Aguire, a counselor from Virginia.

This group is designed to help students:

- Understand the life cycle
- Cope with their personal situations
- Discuss their feelings in a supportive and understanding atmosphere

Group candidates:

- Children who have experienced the death of a parent, relative, sibling, friend, or even a pet
- Four to six students from the same or adjoining grade levels

Group preparation:

Interview each student selected individually and explain the purpose and process of the group. Then send a parent notification and permission letter (page 115).

114

Dear _____,

Death is a traumatic event for every family member. Feelings expressed and not expressed do not go away when the child leaves the house. They are always present and may pop up and become primary at any time during the school day. When this happens, children cannot focus on the tasks being presented in the classroom.

Your child's classroom teacher has identified your child as a student who could benefit from extra help in understanding and coping with a death.

In an effort to help your child and others learn more about this topic, I am forming a counseling group that will focus on helping children cope with deaths that have affected them.

There will be six group meetings scheduled at a time the classroom teacher selects.

Your child knows about the group and has indicated that he or she would like to participate. However, no child is ever included in a small-group counseling program without his or her parents' knowledge and permission.

Please indicate, by completing the form below, that you wish to have your child participate in this group or that you do not want him or her to be included.

Return the permission slip to me by _____.

Thank you,

✂ -

☐ I, _____, *give permission* for my child to participate in the small-group counseling program for children experiencing difficulty in dealing with the death of a loved one.

☐ I, _____, *do not give permission* for my child to participate in the small-group counseling program for children experiencing difficulty in dealing with the death of a loved one.

Child's Name _____ Date _____

School _____ Grade _____

Teacher _____

Home Phone (____) _____ Work Phone (____) _____

Parent's Printed Name _____

Parent's Signature _____

115

INTRODUCTION

Objective:

To help the children understand the goals and rules of the group

Materials Needed:

For each child:
- ☑ Copy of *Group Rules* (page 117)
- ☑ Copy of *Somewhere Over The Rainbow* folder cover (page 118)
- ☑ Pencil
- ☑ Manila folder
- ☑ Crayons or markers
- ☑ Gluestick

For the leader:
- ☑ Dice

Session Preparation:

Reproduce *Group Rules* and the *Somewhere Over The Rainbow* folder cover for each child. Gather any other necessary materials.

Session:

- Roll the dice and tell the children one fact about yourself for each number on the dice. Then have each group member roll the dice and tell one fact about him/herself for each number shown on the dice.

- Explain the purpose of the group to the group members by saying:

   Everyone in this group has lost someone important to him or her. Sometimes it is hard to understand why this important person could not have lived longer. I have lost (<u>IDENTIFY A LOSS YOU HAVE HAD</u>) and have had these same feelings. During our time together, we are going to learn about the natural changes that occur in all living things, our feelings, why memories are important, and how other people can help us. We will celebrate life.

- Distribute a copy of *Group Rules* and a pencil to each child. Explain each rule and its importance. Have each child sign and date his/her copy of *Group Rules* to indicate the child agrees to follow the rules.

- Distribute a manila folder, *Somewhere Over The Rainbow* folder cover, a gluestick, and crayons or markers to each child. Then tell the children that when they arrive each week they will color one section of the rainbow to reflect their progress through the group sessions.

- Have the children select one color and use it to color one segment of the rainbow. When they have finished, they may write their name on their folder and color the other pictures. They should not color in any other sections of the rainbow.

- Have the children glue their folder cover to their manila folder and put their copy of *Group Rules* into the folder.

- Conclude the lesson by collecting the folders and telling the children they will be using the folders in the next session.

GROUP RULES

1
I will respect the privacy of others.

2
I will not tease others or put others down.

3
I will be responsible for and complete homework assigned during group sessions.

4
I will listen when others speak.

5
I will attend each session and arrive on time.

_____   _____
Signature   Date

117

SOMEWHERE OVER THE RAINBOW

NAME

EACH LIVING THING HAS A NATURAL LIFE SPAN

Objective:

To help the children understand the natural changes occurring in the life spans of living things

Materials Needed:

For each child:
- ☑ Child's folder
- ☑ Crayons or markers
- ☑ Drawing paper
- ☑ Styrofoam cup
- ☑ Soil
- ☑ Seeds
- ☑ Pencil
- ☑ Laminated fall leaf

    (*Note:* If fall leaves are not available, you may purchase plastic leaves at a craft store.)

For the leader:
- ☐ None

Session Preparation:

Laminate a fall leaf or purchase a fall leaf for each child in the group. Gather any other necessary materials.

Session:

- Distribute the folders and crayons or markers to the children. Have them color the next segment of the rainbow on their folder cover.

- Distribute a styrofoam cup, seeds, soil, and a pencil to each child. Have the children write their name on the cup, put soil into the cup, and plant one or more seeds in the soil.

- Discuss how the seeds will change and grow to become plants and flowers. Then ask:

    What other living things grow and change? (Trees change from season to season, an egg changes from a chick into a hen, a caterpillar changes into a butterfly, etc.)

- Distribute drawing paper to the children. Have the children divide the paper in half. Ask them to use one half to draw a picture of a living thing that changes.

- Have the children discuss how they themselves have grown and changed since they were born. Now have the children use the other half of the drawing paper to draw a picture of how they have changed since they were born. Allow time for the children to complete their drawings.

- Tell the children that their pictures show that living things grow and change and that these changes are called *life cycles*. Explain that all living things are born, and at the end of their life cycle, all living things die because this is Nature's way.

- Continue the explanation by telling the children that our bodies are wonderful when we gets sick or hurt, because we usually get well or heal. There are times, though, when bodies get too sick or too hurt to get better. And sometimes people live to be very old and their bodies cannot keep living. When these things happen, people die.

- It is important for the children to know that when someone dies, people feel very sad and that this feeling is all right. It is also important for them to know that death is a natural part of the life cycle of all living things, including people.

- Distribute a laminated fall leaf to each child. Tell the children that the leaf has been laminated to preserve its color and is being given to them to remind them that all living things grow and change during their life cycle.

- Conclude the lesson by having the children put their seed cups in a sunny place so they can monitor the changes each week. Tell them to put their drawings into their folders. Collect the folders.

UNDERSTANDING FEELINGS ASSOCIATED WITH DEATH

Objective:

To help children identify, understand, and manage their feelings

Materials Needed:

For each child:
  ☑ Child's folder
  ☑ Copy of *Feelings Faces* (page 123)
  ☑ Copy of *My Feelings* (page 126)
  ☑ Crayons or markers

For the leader:
  ☑ Copy of *Situation Cards*
    (pages 124-125)

Session Preparation:

Reproduce *Feelings Faces* and *My Feelings* for each child and *Situation Cards* for the leader. Gather the other necessary materials.

Session:

• Have the children check on their plants' growth.

• Distribute the folders and crayons or markers to the children. Have them color the next section of the rainbow on their folder cover.

• Distribute *Feelings Faces* to each child. Have the children look at each picture and identify the feeling it expresses. As each feeling is identified, have the children describe when a person may experience that feeling.

• Read each *Situation Card* aloud. After each situation is read, have the children decide which *Feelings Faces* would match each situation. Remind them that a situation could have more than one feeling.

• Distribute *My Feelings* to each child. Tell the children that this is an outline of a person's body. Explain that our feelings are as much a part of us as our nose, eyes, or arms. And just like their arms or noses are neither good nor bad, feelings are neither good nor bad, even though some feelings may make us uncomfortable.

• Ask the children to think about how they feel inside when they are sad. Tell them to think about where inside of them their sad feeling seems to live. When they have decided this, have them use their blue crayon or marker and color the body part on their handout where they feel sadness the most.

• Then have them think about how they feel inside when they are angry. Tell them to decide where inside of them their angry feeling seems to live. When they have decided this, have them use their red crayon or marker and color the body part on their handout where they feel anger the most.

• Repeat this process for the following feelings. Suggested colors are:

    Worried—Orange
    Happy—Yellow
    Relieved—Green
    Scared—Purple

121

- Have each child share the feeling of his/her choice from their activity sheet. Then have the children place both of their activity sheets into their folders.

- Tell the children that when someone we care about dies, we often have lots of these feelings. Sometimes we have more than one feeling at the same time. While this is uncomfortable, it is natural and okay. Feelings will come and go like the waves in the ocean and, as time goes by, the feelings will be like the waves in the ocean—farther and farther apart. You never forget the person you love, but it becomes easier to remember that person without feeling so sad.

- Tell the children some of the things they can do for themselves when they have uncomfortable feelings. Say:

    When you are uncomfortable about the way you are feeling you can talk with people who love you like your friends, family, teachers, and neighbors. Or you can do things you enjoy, like reading, skating, or riding your bike.

(*Note:* At this point, explain that people sometimes feel guilty when they allow themselves to feel enjoyment even though someone they love has died. That is natural, but it is important to remember that feelings and minds need a rest, and that doing things we enjoy is a way to take care of our feelings and our minds. It does not mean that we did not love the person enough or that we don't care.)

- Ask the children to describe some of the feelings they experienced when their important person died. (Allow time for the children to express their feelings if they choose to do so.)

- Conclude the session by giving a homework assignment. Have the children bring in a shoe box or other small box and some memorabilia related to their loved one who has died. The memorabilia could be a picture, a watch, or any remembrance of that person. Tell the children who don't have actual items that they will have a chance to draw pictures of memorabilia to put into their Memory Boxes.

- Collect the folders for the next session.

FEELINGS FACES

RELIEVED

LOVED

SCARED

LONELY

SILLY

HAPPY

SAD

CONFUSED

SHOCKED

MAD

EMBARRASSED

FRUSTRATED

123

You must sing a solo.

Your friend is in the hospital.

Your pet died.

You get to go to the beach.

You have a big test today.

You have to clean your room, wash the car, and take out the trash. All in one day!

You are going to a funeral.

Someone you love hugs you.

Someone hides and
then says, "Boo" to you.

Your parents are crying.

You finished all of your chores and still had time to play.

There is no one to play with.

You make a mistake in front of the whole class and everyone laughs.

Your grandmother is very sick.

You do not understand what the teacher is explaining in math.

MY FEELINGS

MEMORIES HELP US SAY GOOD-BYE

Objective:

To help the children understand the importance memories play in their ability to say "Good-bye"

Materials Needed:

For each child:
- ☑ Child's folder
- ☑ Crayons or markers
- ☑ Drawing paper
- ☑ Shoe box or other small box brought from home
- ☑ Gluestick
- ☑ Materials for decorations (paper, markers, sequins, stickers, etc.)

For the leader:
- ☑ Extra shoe boxes for children who do not bring one from home

(*Note:* An alternative to making *Memory Boxes* would be to make *Memory Balloons* from brightly colored construction paper decorated with pictures drawn with markers or crayons. Yarn is attached to the construction-paper balloons and they are hung on the wall of the counseling office until the final group session.)

Session Preparation:

Gather the necessary materials.

Session:

- Have the children check on their plants' growth.

- Distribute the folders and crayons or markers to the children. Have them color in the next section of the rainbow.

- Tell the children that memories are a very important part of us that no one can ever take away. When someone dies, our many memories of that person will stay with us forever. When someone we love dies, our love for him/her doesn't die. It stays with us as part of our memories of that person. Because we have memories of a person, it is easier to say "Good-bye" to him/her.

- Continue by saying that memories are things we remember from our own experiences with our special person, but that we may also "borrow" memories from other people. For example, our parents may be able to tell us things about our grandparents that can help us feel closer to our grandparents.

- Ask those children who wish to do so to share the "memories" they brought with them. Allow the children time to share with the group items they have brought from home that represent memories of their loved one. Be aware that some children may be suffering because they have few or unclear memories. For example, perhaps a grandfather died when a child was very young and he/she is upset about not getting to know him. Children who do not have items to share, may describe their "memories." Provide drawing paper for them to draw pictures of things they remember and/or were told to them about their special person.

- Tell the children to decorate the boxes they brought from home with the craft materials and gluesticks. Have them put the "memories" relating to their loved one into the boxes.

- Collect the folders for the next session. Conclude this session by allowing the children to take their Memory Boxes home with them.

Objective:

To help the children appreciate the caring community that surrounds them

Materials Needed:

For each child:
- ☑ Child's folder
- ☑ Copy of *My Caring Community* (page 130)
- ☑ Copy of *Paper Dolls* (page 131)
- ☑ Crayons or markers
- ☑ Pencil
- ☑ Scissors

For the leader:
- ☐ None

Session Preparation:

Reproduce *My Caring Community* and *Paper Dolls* for each child. Gather any other necessary materials.

Session:

- Have the children check on their plants' growth. After they have done so, ask:

    How have your plants changed since our first session?

    What do the plants need in order to grow?

    Who helps the plants? (Nature and time help the plants mature and grow. The children have been helping the plants, too.)

- Distribute the folders and crayons or markers to the children. Have them color in the next section of the rainbow on the cover.

- Return the discussion to the plants and tell the children that they helped their plants grow by making sure they had water and enough sun. They even pulled out weeds if needed. Like plants, Nature helps children to grow and change. There are people all around children helping them grow and change. These people teach children things they need to know, make sure they are taken care of, and correct them when they make a mistake. All of this helps children grow strong. These helpers are the people in the children's caring community.

- Distribute *My Caring Community* and a pencil to each child. Have the children write their name in the center of the circle. In the concentric circles surrounding their name, they will write the names of those who care for them. Explain the activity sheet as follows:

    The circle in which you wrote your name represents you. The other circles represent people who care for you. Follow my directions and, when we have finished, you will have a picture of all the people who care about you.

    In the circle closest to yourself, write the names of the family members who live in your home.

    In the next circle, write the names of family members who do not live with you but who still care about you like aunts, uncles, grandparents, etc.

    In the next circle, write the names of close friends and neighbors who care for you. Include other people who care for you like your teacher, counselor, etc.

    In the last circle, write the names of some organizations in your town or world that could assist you if you ever needed help. This could include the Red Cross, certain Hot Lines, etc.

- Tell the children that if they look at their papers, they will see that many people care for them and that all of these people will help them if they ever need someone to talk with or someone to help them with a problem.

- Distribute *Paper Dolls* and scissors to each child. Demonstrate how to fold the paper accordion-style on the dotted lines and how to cut the paper dolls so they all connect. Have the children fold and cut their paper dolls. Then have them write their name on the center figure and write the names of family members and friends on the connecting figures. Tell them that just like the cut-out figures, they are connected to other people who care for them. Remind them that they are never alone.

- Have the children place *My Caring Community* and *Paper Dolls* in their folders. Collect the folders and remind the children that the next session is the final group session.

MY CARING COMMUNITY

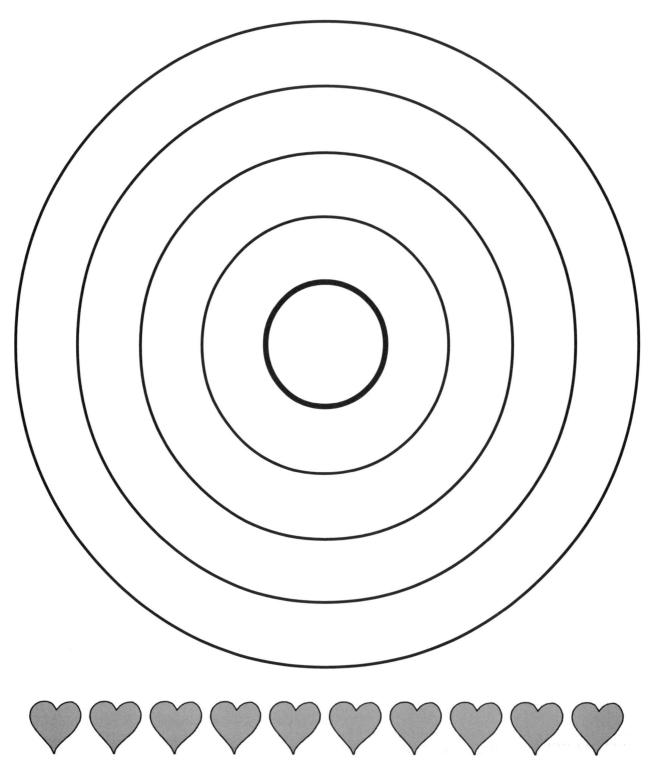

130

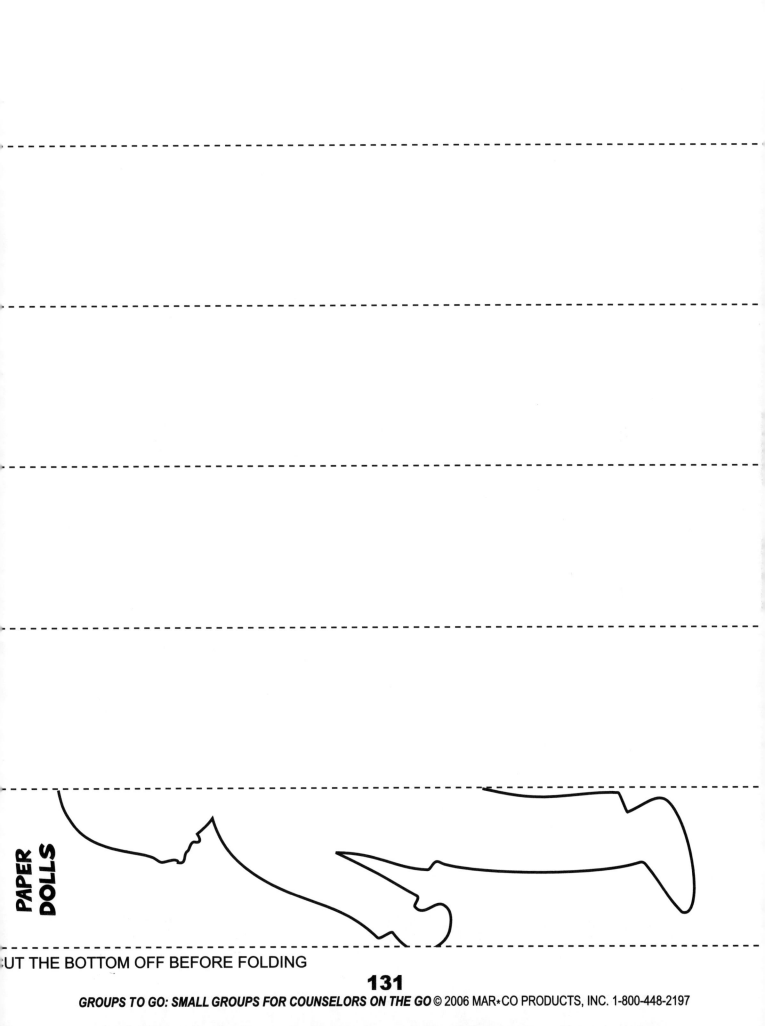

PAPER DOLLS

UT THE BOTTOM OFF BEFORE FOLDING

CELEBRATE LIFE

Objective:

To encourage the children to celebrate life and the people they love

Materials Needed:

For each child:
- ☑ Child's folder
- ☑ Crayons or markers
- ☑ Copy of *The Butterfly* (page 133)
- ☑ Copy of *Somewhere Over The Rainbow* (page 134)

For the leader:
- ☑ Refreshments (Optional)

Session Preparation:

Reproduce *The Butterfly* and *Somewhere Over The Rainbow* for each child. Gather any other necessary materials.

Session:

- Have the children check on their plants' growth.

- Distribute the folders and crayons or markers. Have the children color the last two segments of the rainbow.

- Tell the children that this is the final day of their group. Ask if they remember what their plants were like when they were first planted. Agree with the children that they were tiny seeds that have grown and changed because that is a plant's natural life cycle.

(*Note:* If any of the plants have died over the course of the group, discuss what happened to these plants.)

- Then ask the following questions:

    Do all plants live exactly the same length of time? (No. Some plants live only one year and others come up year after year. Sometimes frost kills plants, etc.)

    Does every seed grow to be a plant? (No. All plants are different and have different life spans. Sometimes things happen to seeds and they die before they can become plants.)

    Will any plant live forever? (No. Every plant will die one day, because plants are living things and all living things die.)

- Continue by telling the children that plants do not live forever because dying is part of Nature. It is impossible to make their plants last forever, but they can enjoy their beauty while they are living. They cannot make people live forever, either. But they can enjoy them and love them while they are alive. That is why memories are so important. Memories of people you love will be with you forever.

- Distribute *The Butterfly* and *Somewhere Over The Rainbow*. Read the poem aloud with the children and discuss its meaning. Then have the children color the butterfly.

(*Note:* This is a good time to share refreshments and reflect on the group experience with the children.)

- Have the children discuss what they enjoyed most about the group, what they would change, and what they learned.

- Have the children add their papers from this session to their folders. Give them their folders and their plants to take home.

THE BUTTERFLY

Walking together, my friend and I
saw a butterfly winging its way to the sky.

"How beautiful," my friend exclaimed.
"Its wings are so bright, they appear to be flames."

The butterfly joined us for part of our walk,
and we were surprised to find it could talk!

"I'm so glad you decided to travel this way,"
said the butterfly on this special day.

"My life is so short, but I'm filled with joy
to meet up with such a nice girl and boy.

"I soar in the sunshine and smile in the rain,
because I may never come this way again!

"I hold all my memories in my heart with great pleasure,
of friends and family, the loved ones I treasure."

We listened as he spoke of how
his life was almost over now.

"Butterflies do not live very long.
We only fly from dawn to dawn.

"Then we flit and we fly,
over the rainbow and into the sky.

"Some friends of mine have already flown,
but I do not feel alone.

"It's Nature's law as you will see,
all things change, but here's the key.

"Spend your life in love and hope,
then with all things you can cope.

"Remember that memories are made every day,
and spend your life living in a joyous way."

Then the bright butterfly turned to the sky,
and over the rainbow we watched him fly.

We wanted to cry, we felt so sad.
But because of his visit, we were really quite glad.

We thought how lucky we were that we heard him say
his message of joy on this wonderful day.

Written by Kaye Aguire

133

SOMEWHERE OVER THE RAINBOW

RESPECT

Self-Respect
Respect For Authority

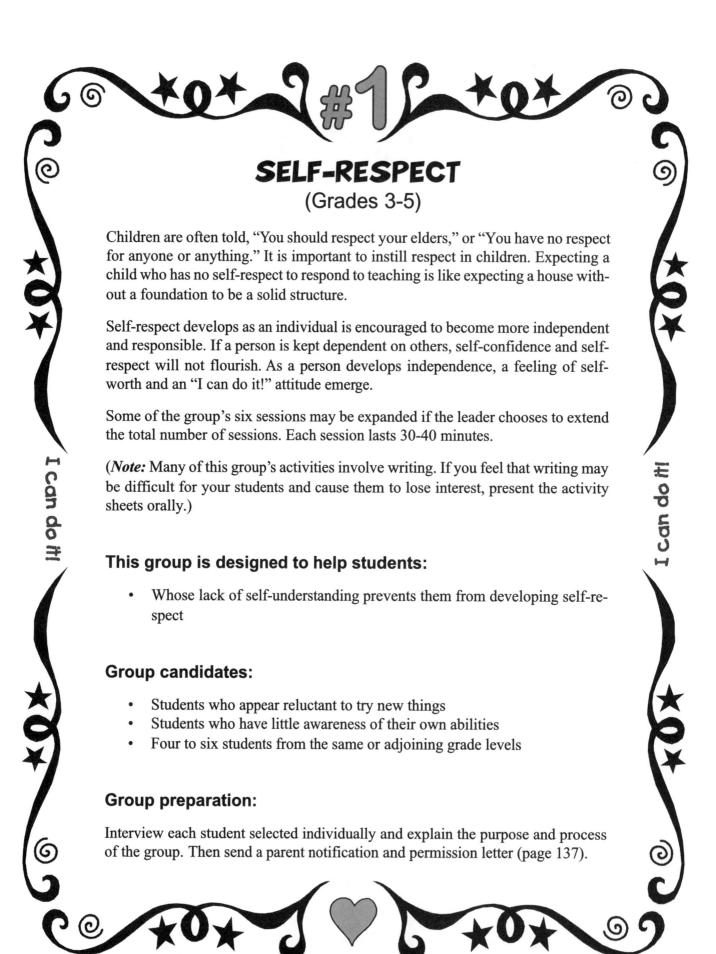

#1

SELF-RESPECT
(Grades 3-5)

Children are often told, "You should respect your elders," or "You have no respect for anyone or anything." It is important to instill respect in children. Expecting a child who has no self-respect to respond to teaching is like expecting a house without a foundation to be a solid structure.

Self-respect develops as an individual is encouraged to become more independent and responsible. If a person is kept dependent on others, self-confidence and self-respect will not flourish. As a person develops independence, a feeling of self-worth and an "I can do it!" attitude emerge.

Some of the group's six sessions may be expanded if the leader chooses to extend the total number of sessions. Each session lasts 30-40 minutes.

(*Note:* Many of this group's activities involve writing. If you feel that writing may be difficult for your students and cause them to lose interest, present the activity sheets orally.)

This group is designed to help students:

- Whose lack of self-understanding prevents them from developing self-respect

Group candidates:

- Students who appear reluctant to try new things
- Students who have little awareness of their own abilities
- Four to six students from the same or adjoining grade levels

Group preparation:

Interview each student selected individually and explain the purpose and process of the group. Then send a parent notification and permission letter (page 137).

Dear _____,

In order to truly respect others, a child must first respect him/herself. Children who are not confident in their abilities and strengths are often unwilling to take part in new academic and social endeavors. Children who do not develop self-respect may experience an unfulfilling adolescence and adulthood.

Your child's classroom teacher has identified your child as a student who could benefit from extra help in developing self-respect.

In an effort to help your child and others learn more about this issue, I am forming a counseling group that will focus on helping children develop self-respect.

There will be six group meetings scheduled at a time the classroom teacher selects.

Your child knows about the group and has indicated that he or she would like to participate. However, no child is ever included in a small-group counseling program without his or her parents' knowledge and permission.

Please indicate, by completing the form below, that you wish to have your child participate in this group or that you do not want him or her to be included.

Return the permission slip to me by _____.

Thank you,

✂ -

☐ I, _____, *give permission* for my child to participate in the small-group counseling program to help children recognize their abilities and develop self-respect.

☐ I, _____, *do not give permission* for my child to participate in the small-group counseling program to help children recognize their abilities and develop self-respect.

Child's Name _____   Date _____

School _____   Grade _____

Teacher _____

Home Phone (_____) _____   Work Phone (_____) _____

Parent's Printed Name _____

Parent's Signature _____

137

Session 1
IMPORTANT TRAITS

Objective:

To help the students determine what traits seem important to them by looking at people they respect

Materials Needed:

For each student:
- ☑ Paper
- ☑ Pencil

For the leader:
- ☑ Chart paper and marker

Session Preparation:

Gather the necessary materials.

Session:

- Beginning with the leader, go around the group and have the students introduce themselves and name two people they admire.

- Give the students a few minutes to think about an answer to this question:

  If you were told you could not be the person you are today but could be any other person, living or dead, who would you choose to be?

- Introduce the word *respect* by explaining that a person we respect is someone we look up to or admire.

- Distribute paper and a pencil to each student. Have the students put their name on their paper and number the page from 1 to 10. Then have them write after each number the name of someone they respect. Tell them that they may list anyone they know or know of: a family member, friend, politician, movie or singing star, TV personality, etc. After each name they list they are to write one thing that they admire about that person.

- Have the students take turns sharing one name from their list and telling what they admire about that person. As the students are contributing their answers, the leader should write the admirable characteristics on the chart paper. Continue having the students share from their lists as long as time allows.

- Conclude the session by labeling the list, *Characteristics We Respect In Others*. Collect the students' papers and save them with the list for the next session.

GROUPS TO GO: SMALL GROUPS FOR COUNSELORS ON THE GO © 2006 MAR*CO PRODUCTS, INC. 1-800-448-2197

ADMIRABLE PERSONAL TRAITS

Objective:

To look at the admirable characteristics we see in ourselves

Materials Needed:

For each student:
- ☑ Paper
- ☑ Pencil

For the leader:
- ☑ *Characteristics We Respect In Others* list from Session 1
- ☑ Student's lists from Session 1

Session Preparation:

Gather the necessary materials.

Session:

- Return the students' lists from the last session. Ask the students to quickly look over their lists.

- Read, or have the students take turns reading, the list of *Characteristics That We Respect In Others.*

- Explain that people are often reluctant to look at the good qualities in themselves. It is easy to put yourself down or look for negative things in yourself. But we are afraid that if we mention positive things about ourselves, others will think we are bragging. However, in order to have self-confidence and self-respect, we must feel good about ourselves.

- Remind the students that during the last session, they listed people they respect and told why they admire them. Explain that in this session, they are going to look at themselves and the good characteristics they possess.

- Distribute paper and a pencil to each student. Have the students put their name on their paper and title their paper *Good Things About Me*. Then have them number the paper from 1 to 10 and, beside each number, write one quality or characteristic they consider to be one of their "strengths."

- Below the list, have them write the heading *Some Weaknesses I Have*. Then have them number the paper from 1 to 3 and, beside each number, write three weaknesses they have and one way they could strengthen each one.

- One at a time, have the students share their list of strengths with the group. After one student finishes and before another begins, have the group members add any strengths the student might not have been mentioned. The student should add these strengths to his/her list.

- Ask those students who are willing to do so to share a weakness from their lists and the way they feel this weakness could be strengthened. As they share their weaknesses, ask the other group members to think of other ways to strengthen them.

- Conclude the lesson by complimenting the students on their openness in identifying their strengths and weaknesses. Collect the students' lists and save them for the final session.

PAST SUCCESSES STRENGTHEN SELF-RESPECT

Objective:

To encourage group members to look at past successes in order to strengthen self-respect

Materials Needed:

For each student:
- ☑ Copy of *My Successes* (page 141)
- ☑ Pencil

For the leader:
- ☑ *Characteristics We Respect In Others* list from Session 1

Session Preparation:

Reproduce *My Successes* for each student. Gather any other necessary materials.

Session:

- Review the *Characteristics That We Respect In Others* list from Session 1.

- Tell the students that self-respect and self-confidence are built on past successes. When students perform effectively in academic areas, in sports or physical skills, or in relationships with others, self-confidence increases and that leads to increased self-respect.

- Distribute *My Successes* and a pencil to each student. Have the students complete the sheet, then share one academic success they experienced and tell how they felt after having achieving success. Then proceed to physical success, following the same procedure. Finally, have the students share their successful relationships with others.

- Have the group members write an answer to the following statement on the bottom of their papers:

  When I do something successful, I feel _____ about myself.

  Then ask the students to share their responses with the group.

- Collect the students' sheets and save them for the final session.

- Conclude the group by saying:

  You must believe in yourself in order to be truly successful. When you are successful, you will gain self-confidence and self-confidence leads to self-respect.

Name_____ Date_____

 # MY SUCCESSES

List some of your past successes in each of the following areas.

Academics

1. _____

_____

2. _____

_____

3. _____

_____

Physical Skills or Sports Activities

1. _____

_____

2. _____

_____

3. _____

_____

Relationships With Others

1. _____

_____

2. _____

_____

3. _____

_____

When I do something successful, I feel _____ about myself.

Session 4
ACCEPTING RESPONSIBILITIES STRENGTHENS SELF-RESPECT

Objective:

To help group members understand the relationship between accepting responsibilities and self-respect

Materials Needed:

Foe each student:
☐ None

For the leader:
☑ Chalkboard and chalk or chart paper and marker

Session Preparation:

Gather the necessary materials.

Session:

• Ask each student to take a trip into the past and recall the first thing he/she can remember. This should be something the student remembers, not something someone told him/her. Have each student describe his/her memory and how old he/she was when the event occurred.

• List the different ages on the board/chart paper. Then ask the students to think of different responsibilities they successfully handled at different ages in their lives. List all age levels up to and including the present age of the group members.

A list might include:

Three to Four Years (Nursery School): Put on socks and shoes, picked up toys, came when called, etc.

Five Years (Kindergarten): Tied shoes, finished a seatwork paper, zipped coat, etc.

Six Years (First Grade): Read and finished workbook pages, made bed, bought own lunch, etc.

Seven, Eight, Nine, Ten Years (Second-Fifth Grade): Wrote original stories, completed projects for Scouts, fed and cared for pets, did homework, etc.)

(*Note:* When having the students do this, complete one year at a time.)

• After the group members have had input into each age level of responsibility, present the following statements. Ask each student to give his/her opinion about each statement. Say:

People who get others to take over responsibilities they can handle do not have as much self-respect as those who handle responsibilities they are capable of handling.

The more responsibilities you are able to handle, the more positive feelings you gain about yourself.

Responsibility should increase with age. Small children don't have as many responsibilities as adults.

You should assume responsibility for more and more difficult jobs as you grow toward adulthood.

- Then ask the students the following questions:

    How do you feel when you do a good job on a task? Why?

    Why do some people try to get out of doing certain tasks?

    Why would these people have or not have strong self-respect or self-confidence? (They would not have strong self-confidence because they would never know whether they really could have done the task. They might think they could have done it if they had wanted to, but they would not know for sure. Not doing tasks that others your age do hinders self-respect.)

- Conclude the session by asking the students to think about things they are capable of doing but do not do at home and at school. If these are tasks they have been asked to do, such as cleaning their room or finishing assignments, tell them to pick one to do at home and one at school and do them until the next session.

Session 5
MAKING DECISIONS HELPS DEVELOP SELF-RESPECT

Objective:

To show how decisions made in accordance with the students' value system help them develop self-respect

Materials Needed:

For each student:
- ☑ Copy of *Situation Sheet #1* (page 145)
- ☑ Copy of *Situation Sheet #2* (page 146)
- ☑ Copy of *Situation Sheet #3* (page 147)
- ☑ Pencil

For the leader:
- ☐ None

Session Preparation:

Reproduce *Situation Sheet #1, Situation Sheet #2,* and *Situation Sheet #3* for each student. Gather any other necessary materials.

Session:

- Distribute the three situation sheets and a pencil to each student. Without any discussion, have the students complete the three sheets.

- Discuss the students' answers to the questions on each situation sheet. Have the group come to a consensus about which choice each student in the situation sheets would make. Then ask:

  Why do you think (NAME OF STUDENT) made this choice?

  What character trait did (NAME OF STUDENT) have that influences this choice?

  Who do you think might have influenced the choice? (Parents, friends, etc.)

- Conclude the session by asking the students:

  Do you think character traits influence self-respect?

  Tell the students that having good or positive character traits increase self-respect.

- Collect the students' sheets and save them for the final session.

SITUATION SHEET #1

Situation: Tom goes back to pick up a book he left in science class. His teacher, Mr. Jones, is working at his desk. Tom stops to talk with him. As they are talking, Mr. Jones is called to the office. As Tom looks over Mr. Jones' desk, he notices that the unit science test with the answer key has been left out in full view.

What are Tom's two choices?

CHOICE #1 _____

What effect will this choice have on others? _____

_____

_____

_____

What effect will this choice have on Tom's self-respect?

_____

_____

_____

CHOICE #2 _____

What effect will this choice have on others? _____

_____

_____

_____

What effect will this choice have on Tom's self-respect?

_____

_____

_____

Name_____   Date_____

SITUATION SHEET #2

Situation: Sue is walking home from her friend's house. As she passes the church on the corner, she notices three boys she knows from school throwing rocks at the church windows.

What are Sue's two choices?

CHOICE #1 _____

What effect will this choice have on others? _____

_____

_____

_____

What effect will this choice have on Sue's self-respect?

_____

_____

_____

CHOICE #2 _____

What effect will this choice have on others? _____

_____

_____

_____

What effect will this choice have on Sue's self-respect?

_____

_____

_____

SITUATION SHEET #3

Situation: Joyce goes to the shopping mall with three of her girlfriends. They walk around having a good time, looking in store windows at clothes and discussing what they wish they could buy. The other three girls then begin to talk about what they plan to shoplift when they get to the drugstore.

What are Joyce's two choices?

CHOICE #1 _____

What effect will this choice have on others? _____

_____

_____

_____

What effect will this choice have on Joyce's self-respect?

_____

_____

_____

CHOICE #2 _____

What effect will this choice have on others? _____

_____

_____

_____

What effect will this choice have on Joyce's self-respect?

_____

_____

_____

HELPING OTHERS DEVELOPS SELF-RESPECT

Objective:

To show students that by helping others develop self-confidence and self-respect, they will improve their own self-confidence and self-respect

Materials Needed:

Foe each student:
- ☑ Copy of *Helping Others Feel Confident* (page 149)
- ☑ Pencil
- ☑ Manila folder or piece of construction paper

For the leader:
- ☐ None

Session Preparation:

Reproduce *Helping Others Feel Confident* for each student. Gather any other necessary materials.

Session:

- Distribute *Helping Others Feel Confident* and a pencil to each student. Tell the students that as they help others develop self-confidence, they become more self-confident as well. This, in turn, elevates their self-respect. In order to help another person feel confident, they must communicate their belief and faith in that person's ability to handle various situations.

- Have the students complete the sheet.

- Discuss each situation, having the students answer the question:

    How did helping others develop self-confidence make you feel better about yourself?

- Conclude the group by returning all the papers from the previous sessions. Distribute a manila folder or construction paper to the students for a cover. Have them label their cover *Self-Respect*. Thank the students for their cooperation during the sessions and suggest they re-read their responses from time to time to refresh their memories of the ways to improve self-respect in themselves and others.

Name_____   Date_____

HELPING OTHERS FEEL CONFIDENT

Directions: Write what you would say in the following situations to help the other person feel confident.

Situation #1: Your best friend must give a talk in front of the whole grade level. She says, "I'm really scared. A lot of the kids know more about this topic than I do."

What would you say to your friend? _____

_____

_____

Situation #2: Your brother is running the 100-yard dash in a track meet tomorrow. The runner with the best time recorded for this event will be running against him. He tells you, "I might as well skip the race tomorrow. I can't possibly win."

How would you respond to him? _____

_____

_____

Situation #3: You are captain of your baseball team, and you must pick the first nine players to begin the game. Your friend tells you he/she hopes to be chosen to start the game. He/She is not one of the nine starters you chose.

How do you respond to your friend without destroying his/her self-confidence?

_____

_____

_____

149

RESPECT FOR AUTHORITY
(Grades 4-5)

Lack of respect for authority is a major problem in today's schools. Teachers feel the lack of respect in their classrooms and they hear the lack of respect when listening to young people talk about their parents and society. Is this really lack of respect or are young people just wishing to identify with the independence and rebellion that are part of growing up? This question may be answered by exploring the issue in the six-session small-group counseling program *Respect For Authority*.

This group is designed to help students:

- Understand the meaning of *authority* and identify authority figures
- Understand why they make certain decisions
- Identify alternatives students may use
- Determine who can help them evaluate various alternatives
- Evaluate the end results of various alternatives before making final decisions.

Group candidates:

- Students who have problems respecting authority figures
- Students who show respect only for their own gains
- Four to six students from the same or adjoining grade levels

Group preparation:

Interview each student selected individually and explain the purpose and process of the group. Then send a parent notification and permission letter (page 151).

Dear _____,

Behaving respectfully toward adults is an important part of developing good character. Children do not often see any point in being respectful to adults inside or outside the home. They do not recognize the importance of authority figures and show little regard for the jobs authority figures are trying to do.

Your child's classroom teacher has identified your child as a student who could benefit from extra help in learning to respect authority figures.

In an effort to help your child and others learn more about respect, I am forming a counseling group that will focus on helping children understand the importance of authority figures.

There will be six group meetings scheduled at a time the classroom teacher selects.

Your child knows about the group and has indicated that he or she would like to participate. However, no child is ever included in a small-group counseling program without his or her parents' knowledge and permission.

Please indicate, by completing the form below, that you wish to have your child participate in this group or that you do not want him or her to be included.

Return the permission slip to me by _____.

Thank you,

✂ -

☐ I, _____, ***give permission*** for my child to participate in the small-group counseling program about respectful behavior.

☐ I, _____, ***do not give permission*** for my child to participate in the small-group counseling program about respectful behavior.

Child's Name _____ Date _____

School _____ Grade _____

Teacher _____

Home Phone (____) _____ Work Phone (____) _____

Parent's Printed Name _____

Parent's Signature _____

151

AUTHORITY: WHAT IS IT AND WHO HAS IT?

Objective:

To introduce and discuss vocabulary words related to authority and authority figures

Materials Needed:

For each student:
☐ None

For each student group:
☑ Paper
☑ Pencil

For the leader:
☑ Chart paper and marker

Session Preparation:

Gather the necessary materials.

Session:

•   Write the words *officer, influence, ruler,* and *command* on the chart paper.

•   Divide the students into groups of two or three students. Give each group paper and a pencil. Assign one or two of the words written on the chart paper to each group.

•   Tell the students they will have five minutes to list as many words as they can think of that are associated with the word(s) assigned to them. Have each group choose a recorder to write down its suggestions.

152

- When the allotted time has elapsed, have each group share its words and write them beside their assigned words listed on the chart paper.

- Discuss the word *officer* and the associated words selected by the students. Then tell the students that officers are usually thought of as leaders and people in management positions. The officers in the armed services, the officers of a company, and law enforcement officers are all people who have the responsibility to carry out certain duties of leadership.

- Discuss the word *influence* and the associated words selected by the students. Then tell the students that when thinking about the word *influence*, they should also think about the words *control, power,* and *prestige*. Influential people often have the power to control other people in some manner. Whether they have prestige depends on the manner in which they conduct themselves.

- Continue with the word *ruler* by explaining that a ruler can be a person who is in charge, like a teacher, president, or king. Others look up to these people because of their knowledge.

- Finish with the word *command,* making sure the students understand that it is associated with the words *control, dominate, power,* and *rule.*

- Ask the students to look at the four words and their associated words and list people they know whom they feel would fit into each category. Tell the students that each group should work together as before, but that this time, they will associate people with all four words. A name may be used with more than one word. For example, a teacher's name or a famous general's name may fit with more than one word. Give the students about five minutes to complete the task.

- When the allotted time has elapsed, have the groups share their names. Record them on the chart paper. Tell the students that all of the words they have thought of during this session are related to one word, and that all of the people they thought of during the last activity are related to two words.

- On the chart paper, write the words *authority* and *authority figure*. Review how each of the four words the students worked with at the beginning of the session is related to the word *authority*. Then have the students explain why each name listed is an *authority figure*.

- Conclude the session by telling the students that during the remaining the sessions, they will be discussing authority and authority figures, their feelings about authority figures, and the way they relate to authority figures.

- Save the authority-figure list for future sessions.

DO WE NEED AUTHORITY FIGURES?

Objective:

To help the students realize the importance of authority figures in our society

Materials Needed:

For each student:
☐ None

For each student group:
☑ Art paper
☑ Crayons or markers

For the leader:
☑ Chalkboard and chalk or
   chart paper and marker
☑ Authority-figure list from Session 1

Session Preparation:

Gather the necessary materials.

Session:

•   Referring to the list from Session 1, review the names of the identified authority figures. Ask the students to add any other names they feel should be included in the list.

•   Divide the students into equal groups. Assign each group an authority figure from the list. Then give each group a piece of art paper and crayons or markers.

•   Tell the students they will have 15 minutes to work together and draw a picture of what their world would be like if these authority figures did not exist.

•   When the allotted time has elapsed, have each group share its picture. Then ask the following question:

    Are authority figures necessary? (**Note:** It may be necessary to tell the students that the question of whether they are necessary has nothing to do with whether the students like them.)

•   Allow time for the students to answer the question. Their comments may be written on the board/chart paper.

•   Conclude the session when the students agree that authority figures are necessary.

WHAT IS RESPECT?

Objective:

To have the students analyze the role of the authority figure in society

Materials Needed:

For each student:
- ☐ None

For the leader:
- ☑ Chalkboard and chalk or chart paper and marker
- ☑ Authority-figure list from Session 1

Session Preparation:

Write the following statements on the board/chart paper. These statements summarize the concepts previously presented.

An *authority* is someone who has a great deal of knowledge about a subject.

An *authority figure* is someone who has control or power over others.

Authority figures are necessary in our society.

Gather any other necessary materials.

Session:

- Referring to the board/chart paper, review the concepts previously presented.

- Introduce the topic of *respect* by writing the following dictionary definition on the board/chart paper.

    Respect implies recognizing and honoring the worth of someone or something.

- Ask the students to read the definition, then answer the following questions:

    Does the definition say that respect *means agreeing with the person?* (No.)

    Does the definition say that respect *means liking the person?* (No.)

- When it is understood that the answers to both of the above questions is "no," ask:

    What do you believe the phrase respect for authority *means?* (Lead the discussion to the conclusion that *respect for authority* means appreciating the person for the job he/she does. Emphasize that you need not agree with or like an authority figure in order to respect him/her.)

- Return to the list of authority figures named in Session 1. Review each one, asking the students to identify what job each does and why that person deserves respect.

    For example:

    Police officers are authority figures whose job it is to stop crimes. They deserve respect for putting their lives on the line to help make us safe.

Teachers are authority figures whose job is to educate students. They deserve respect for learning how to do this and passing knowledge on to students.

Parents are authority figures whose job is to raise children to be responsible adults. They deserve respect for devoting years of their lives to seeing that their children can function productively in the world.

• Conclude the session by telling the students they have done a great job of recognizing the worth of the authority figures they named. They should remember that no one is perfect and authority figures sometimes make mistakes. Emphasize that they should be very careful not to disrespect all authority figures because one or two may make a mistake. It is important they look at the complete picture and be as fair to authority figures as they want authority figures to be to them.

AUTHORITY FIGURES: WHAT'S THE PROBLEM?

Objective:

To analyze why some authority figures are accepted and others are not

Materials Needed:

For each student:
☐ None

For the leader:
☑ Chalkboard and chalk or chart paper and marker

Session Preparation:

Gather the necessary materials.

Session:

- Review the concept that authority figures should be respected for the jobs they do.

- Draw two columns on the board/chart paper. Label one column *Acceptable* and the other *Unacceptable*. Then tell the students to think about the authority figures they know and those they have heard of. Remind them that there are authority figures in the world and that everyone must associate with them at certain times.

- Have the students identify the behaviors, without naming names, that allow some authority figures to be accepted while others are rejected. Write the students' reasons in the appropriate column.

- After about 10 minutes, review the lists with the students. Then ask them why these behaviors are acceptable or unacceptable.

- Using the positive and negative lists, have the students give examples of their reactions to authority figures' behaviors. Have them cite specific incidents and tell exactly what their feelings were and how they reacted.

If needed, give the students the following examples:

A teacher sees you doing something that is against the school rules. The teacher yells at you and tells you to stop or you will be sent to the principal. You feel angry because the teacher yelled at you. You do what the teacher says, but only because you are told to, not because you feel what you were doing was wrong.

A teacher sees you doing something that is against the school rules. The teacher walks up to you, asks what you are doing, and asks if you are aware of the consequences if you are sent to the principal. You feel upset because you were caught. You answer the teacher's questions and stop the misbehavior because you know it is going to get you into trouble.

- Continue this train of thought by telling the students that the incident is the same in both examples, but the teacher, who is an authority figure, handled the situation differently.

In the first case, the teacher yelled and threatened. In the second case, the teacher asked questions that made the misbehaving student think about the action and its possible consequences.

- List the student's examples of their reactions to authority figures' behaviors on the board/chart paper. Write the key words that explain reasons for negative or positive feelings toward the authority figure.

- After the students have given their examples, review the listed words. Divide the words into two categories, those that promote a "good attitude" and those that promote a "poor attitude." Review the two groups of words.

- Conclude the session by telling the students that it is easy to like an authority figure who leaves you with a positive feeling, but more difficult to like an authority figure who leaves you with a negative feeling. Remind the students that it is not necessary to agree with or like authority figures in order to respect them.

158

GETTING ALONG WITH AUTHORITY FIGURES

Objective:

To help students understand the purpose of and strategies for getting along with authority figures

Materials Needed:

For each student:
☐ None

For each student group:
☑ Copy of *Getting Along With An Authority Figure* (page 160)
☑ Pencil

For the leader:
☐ None

Session Preparation:

Reproduce *Getting Along With An Authority Figure* for each student group. Gather any other necessary materials.

Session:

• Review, from Session 4, the concept that it is difficult to accept an authority figure who leaves you with a negative feeling.

• Remind the students that the definition of *respect* does not say they must agree with or like the authority figure.

• Divide the students into groups. Have each group select a recorder. Give each group *Getting Along With An Authority Figure* and a pencil. Tell each group to read the situation and, as a group, answer the questions.

• When the groups have completed the task, have each group share its answers with the others. After each group has shared its answers, tell the students that if they seem to have difficulty with a teacher, they should remember that teachers deserve respect for the knowledge they impart. Students who wish to learn must remember that the knowledge they gain is more important than the relationship they think they should have with the teacher.

• Ask the students to describe difficulties they have had with school authority figures. (The leader may choose to or choose not to allow the students to mention names.) As each situation is related, have the student answer the same questions as those answered on the activity sheet. As the students make their contributions and answer the questions, the idea of *getting along for the sake of learning* will be reinforced.

• Conclude the session by reminding the students that in order for them to learn, their primary task is to respect the authority figures (teachers) for the knowledge they have and put personal feelings in a secondary position.

Name_____   Date_____

GETTING ALONG WITH AN AUTHORITY FIGURE

SITUATION: Your teacher constantly picks on you. She calls on you each day with a question you cannot often answer. When you are able to answer the question, she makes a comment about being amazed you could do it. When you are not able to answer the question, she makes a comment about not expecting you to know the answer.

Who is the authority figure? _____

What do you respect about this person? _____

_____

_____

Is it possible for you to like this person? _____

How do you feel about this person? _____

_____

Do you need to like this person in order to respect her? _____

What does this person expect you to do? _____

_____

_____

What can you do to get along with this person? _____

_____

_____

_____

_____

GROUPS TO GO: SMALL GROUPS FOR COUNSELORS ON THE GO © 2006 MAR✳CO PRODUCTS, INC. 1-800-448-2197

...RESULT IS MOST IMPORTANT

result would be if they cooperated with the authority figure and what the end result would be if they did not cooperate.

- When the groups have finished, have each present its situation and conclusions to the others. After each conclusion is presented, ask the students the following questions so they will see that it is important for them to show respect for authority figures:

    Who gets hurt by not respecting an authority figure? (The child gets hurt.)

    In what way does the child lose? (Accept any appropriate answer.)

    Who benefits by respecting an authority figure? (The child benefits.)

    In what way does the child win? (Accept any appropriate answer.)

Session:

- Tell the students that this is their final session. Explain that in this session, it is important that they view their relationships with authority figures not by what is happening now, but by what the end result will be if they do not cooperate with the authority figure.

- Return to the list of authority figures compiled in Session 1. Divide the students into groups. Tell each group to select, from the list, an authority figure they can relate to in a real situation. Each group must select a different authority figure. Each group should discuss its situation and decide what the end

- Conclude the group by telling the students that during the previous sessions, they learned how valuable respect for authority is and what they must do in order to get along with authority figures. Emphasize that the rest is up to them, as they will be making choices every day about their future as they decide how to handle difficult situations with authority figures. If they choose to be in conflict, they will be hurting themselves. If they choose to cooperate, they will be helping themselves. This group has taught them the skills they need. Now the choice is up to them.

SELF-CONFIDENCE

Developing
Self-Confidence Through Drama

Human Relationships And
Self-Confidence

DRAMA CAN BUILD SELF-CONFIDENCE
(Grades 3-5)

What makes one student eager to stand in front of the class and give a book report and another hope he/she never has to do it? What makes one student ready and eager to try new things and another want to stay with what he/she knows? The answer is *self-confidence*.

Lack of self-confidence can hold a student back academically and socially. As that student grows into adulthood, the lack of self-confidence can hold him/her back in personal relationships as well as in a career.

Drama Can Build Self-Confidence is designed to stimulate creativity, imagination, and self-expression. The goal of the group is for the students to rewrite a familiar fairy tale and present it to a group of younger students. Each group member will role-play a character and evaluate his/her performance. Performing in front of an audience will help students develop poise and self-confidence.

This group is designed to help students:

- Who are shy and withdrawn or disruptive, and those who fall between these two extremes

Group candidates:

- Students who deviate from the behavior norm; showing little or no self-confidence through withdrawal or being disruptive
- Six to eight students from the same or adjoining grade levels

Group preparation:

Interview each student selected individually and explain the purpose and process of the group. Then send a parent notification and permission letter (page 165).

Dear _____,

Self-confidence is the cornerstone for building relationships, academic success, and positive decision making. Students who display a lack of self-confidence can be easily led or isolated by peers, perfectionistic or afraid to take any risk, or fearful of making decisions.

Your child's classroom teacher has identified your child as a student who could benefit from extra help in developing self-confidence.

In an effort to help your child and others learn more about this issue, I am forming a counseling group that will focus on helping children develop self-confidence.

There will be six group meetings scheduled at a time the classroom teacher selects.

Your child knows about the group and has indicated that he or she would like to participate. However, no child is ever included in a small-group counseling program without his or her parents' knowledge and permission.

Please indicate, by completing the form below, that you wish to have your child participate in this group or that you do not want him or her to be included.

Return the permission slip to me by _____.

Thank you,

✂ -

☐ I, _____, *give permission* for my child to participate in the small-group counseling program for improving self-confidence.

☐ I, _____, *do not give permission* for my child to participate in the small-group counseling program for improving self-confidence.

Child's Name _____ Date _____

School _____ Grade _____

Teacher _____

Home Phone (____) _____ Work Phone (____) _____

Parent's Printed Name _____

Parent's Signature _____

Objective:

To help group members get to know each other and perform a simple dramatic task without speaking

Materials Needed:

For each student:
- ☐ None

For the leader:
- ☑ Large box or bag
- ☑ Blindfold
- ☑ Variety of props
  (hats, baggy pants, skirts, coats, baseball bat, tennis racket, football, jewelry, old fur, apron, etc.)

Session Preparation:

Gather the necessary materials and place all the props, except the blindfold, in the large box/bag.

Session:

- Have the students introduce themselves and name their favorite TV show and their favorite fairy tale.

- Divide the group into two teams. Have each team choose a captain. Each captain should be blindfolded and, in turn, draw three or four items from the prop box. Have the captains take the items to their teams.

- Tell the students that it is the job of each team to make up a skit using no words (like a silent movie) and incorporate all team members and their chosen props in the skit. The skit should be approximately two minutes long.

- Tell the students they have 10 minutes to prepare the skit.

- When the allotted time has elapsed, have each team present its drama for the other team.

- After each drama has been presented, the opposite team should guess what was being presented.

- Discuss the importance of body language, facial expressions, movement, etc. in getting across a drama without speaking.

- Conclude the session by having each team make three positive statements about the other team's presentation.

Objective:

To help the students understand how spoken language enhances a dramatic presentation.

Materials Needed:

For each student:
☐ None

For the leader:
☑ Large box or bag
☑ Blindfold
☑ Variety of props
(hats, baggy pants, skirts, coats,
baseball bat, tennis racket, football,
jewelry, old fur, apron, etc.)

Session Preparation:

Gather the necessary materials and place all the props, except the blindfold, in the large box/bag.

Session:

• Ask the students how they felt when they created and presented their skits in the last session.

• Divide the students into the same two teams. Have each team choose a different captain. Each captain should be blindfolded and, in turn, draw three or four items from the prop box. Have the captains take the items to their teams.

• Tell the students that each team will have 10 minutes to make up a skit approximately two minutes long and will present it to the other team. The skits must include the props and each team member. This time words may be used.

• When the allotted time has elapsed, have each team present its drama for the other team.

• After the presentations, discuss how speaking made the skits more interesting and easier to understand.

• Conclude the session by having each team make three positive statements about the other team's presentation.

WRITING A DRAMATIZATION

Objective:

To teach the students to work together cooperatively and begin to use their creativity

Materials Needed:

For the student group:
- ☑ Paper
- ☑ Pencil

For the leader:
- ☐ None

Session Preparation:

Gather the necessary materials.

Session:

- Have one student briefly tell the story of Cinderella or have the students tell the story cooperatively as a group.

- Explain that there are different versions of this story. Read or tell the following version to the group.

  ### CINDER-ELWOOD

  Cinder-Elwood lived with his stepfather and his two stepbrothers. His stepfather was not very kind to him. His stepbrothers were very large boys. They insisted on getting their own way and often pushed Cinder-Elwood around. When there were jobs to be done around the yard and house, Cinder-Elwood always ended up

doing them. Cinder-Elwood was shy and quiet and didn't get along too well with his two stepbrothers. All three boys went to the same school, and Cinder-Elwood often had to carry his stepbrothers' books and lunches.

The two stepbrothers came home one day and announced that they were going to try out for the baseball team. Cinder-Elwood loved baseball and wanted very much to try out, too. As Cinder-Elwood mowed the large lawn and watched his stepbrothers practice baseball, he did not think he could ever make the team.

One day, his grandmother came to visit him. She wanted to know why Cinder-Elwood looked so sad …

- Pause at this point and discuss how the characters in this story are similar to those in the original story.

- Explain that the students are going to put on a dramatization based on the Cinderella plot. They may complete the Cinder-Elwood story or compose a different version of their own. Tell the students that there must be a part in the dramatization for each group member.

- All the students' ideas should be considered before the group decides on the best one and creates at least an outline for the dramatization.

- Distribute paper and a pencil to the group. Have the students choose a recorder and work together on this task for the rest of the session.

- Conclude the session by collecting the outline.

DEVELOPING THE DRAMATIZATION

Objective:

To help the students learn to work together creatively and make group decisions.

Materials Needed:

For each student:
  ☐ None

For the leader:
  ☑ Outline of the dramatization from Session 3
  ☑ Props from Session 1

Session Preparation:

Gather the necessary materials.

Session:

• Return the outline to the group. If the dramatization is not complete, have the students complete it at this time. If it is complete, the group must decide who will play each part. If several people want the same parts, try-outs for those parts may be held with the rest of the group choosing the person who best portrays that part. Remind the students that there must be a part for each group member. If there are not enough characters in the story, more characters must be added. These characters could be an announcer, other family members, etc.

• After all parts are assigned, each student must decide which of the props from the prop box would most enhance his/her part. (*Note:* Some group decision making may be required.)

• Conclude the group by having the students begin rehearsing their skit, starting at the opening of the story. The leader should make suggestions to the actors as needed. The students may also have suggestions.

FINALIZING THE DRAMATIZATION

Objective:

To help the students develop self-confidence through drama

Materials Needed:

For each student:
☐ None

For the leader:
☑ Props from Session 1

Session Preparation:

Gather the necessary materials. Arrange for Session 6 to be a presentation of the drama to a group of younger students.

Session:

• Tell the students that at the next and final session they will be presenting their skit to the _____ grade class. This session will be their last opportunity for rehearsal.

• Spend the rest of the session rehearsing the dramatization. The leader will make suggestions to improve the weaker parts of the production.

• Conclude the lesson by telling the students that you are looking forward to the next session, when they will be presenting their work to a _____ grade class.

PRESENTING THE DRAMATIZATION

Objective:

To help the students build self-confidence by presenting their dramatization to another class

Materials Needed:

For each student:
☐ None

For the leader:
☑ Props from Session 1

Session Preparation:

Gather the necessary materials.

Session:

• Have the students present the skit to the selected class.

• After the presentation, have the group members write an evaluation of or discuss their own performance. Do this by asking:

Did you think you might forget your part?

Were you nervous before or during the skit?

Do you think you learned something by presenting this skit? If so, what?

Would you like to do other dramatic presentations in the future?

• Conclude the group by thanking the students for their participation.

171

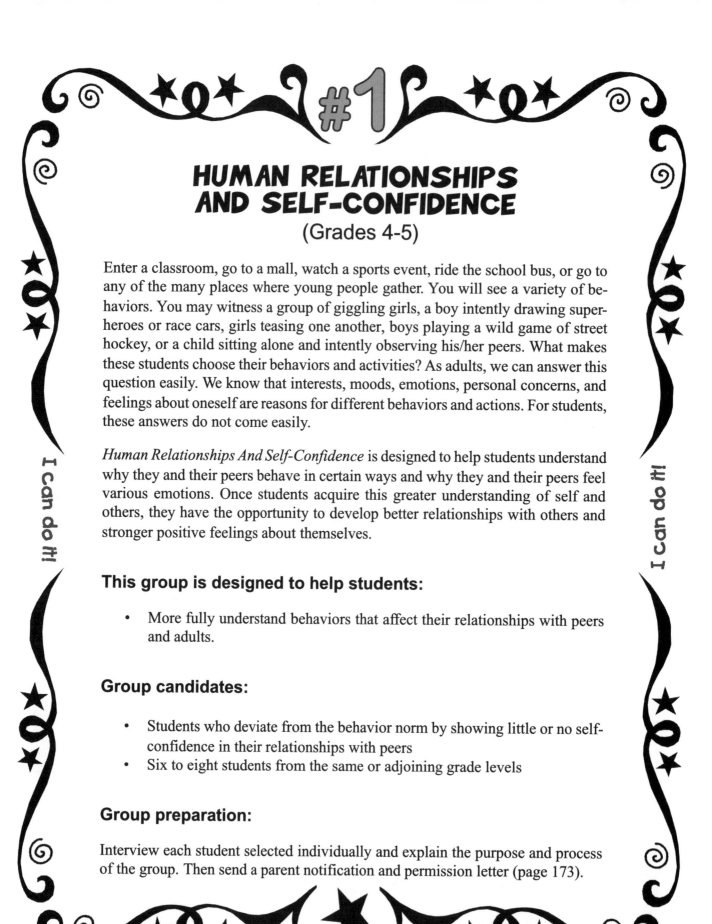

#1

HUMAN RELATIONSHIPS AND SELF-CONFIDENCE
(Grades 4-5)

Enter a classroom, go to a mall, watch a sports event, ride the school bus, or go to any of the many places where young people gather. You will see a variety of behaviors. You may witness a group of giggling girls, a boy intently drawing superheroes or race cars, girls teasing one another, boys playing a wild game of street hockey, or a child sitting alone and intently observing his/her peers. What makes these students choose their behaviors and activities? As adults, we can answer this question easily. We know that interests, moods, emotions, personal concerns, and feelings about oneself are reasons for different behaviors and actions. For students, these answers do not come easily.

Human Relationships And Self-Confidence is designed to help students understand why they and their peers behave in certain ways and why they and their peers feel various emotions. Once students acquire this greater understanding of self and others, they have the opportunity to develop better relationships with others and stronger positive feelings about themselves.

This group is designed to help students:

- More fully understand behaviors that affect their relationships with peers and adults.

Group candidates:

- Students who deviate from the behavior norm by showing little or no self-confidence in their relationships with peers
- Six to eight students from the same or adjoining grade levels

Group preparation:

Interview each student selected individually and explain the purpose and process of the group. Then send a parent notification and permission letter (page 173).

172

Dear _____,

As children grow older, peer influence accelerates. Children who have difficulty relating to their peer group also have low self-confidence. This combination can cause hurt, insecurity, and confusion. Children who carry this burden may never realize their academic or social potential.

Your child's classroom teacher has identified your child as a student who could benefit from extra help in learning to relate better to peers and, in turn, develop greater self-confidence.

In an effort to help your child and others learn more about this issue, I am forming a counseling group that will focus on helping children develop self-confidence.

There will be six group meetings scheduled at a time the classroom teacher selects.

Your child knows about the group and has indicated that he or she would like to participate. However, no child is ever included in a small-group counseling program without his or her parents' knowledge and permission.

Please indicate, by completing the form below, that you wish to have your child participate in this group or that you do not want him or her to be included.

Return the permission slip to me by _____.

Thank you,

- -

☐ I, _____, ***give permission*** for my child to participate in the small-group counseling program for improving self-confidence.

☐ I, _____, ***do not give permission*** for my child to participate in the small-group counseling program for improving self-confidence.

Child's Name _____   Date _____

School _____   Grade _____

Teacher _____

Home Phone (_____) _____   Work Phone (_____) _____

Parent's Printed Name _____

Parent's Signature _____

EVERYONE WANTS TO BELONG

Objective:

To help children learn about the basic need to belong and how the body reacts when this need is not met

Materials Needed:

For each student:
☐ None

For the leader:
☑ Rubber playground ball

Session Preparation:

Gather the necessary materials.

Session:

- Ask one student to volunteer for a special activity. Have the volunteer leave the room while you discuss the activity with the other group members.

- Tell the students they are going to play a game of ball similar to "Keep Away" and that they are to pass the ball to everyone except the one person who is out of the room. Tell them to be sure that each of them has the opportunity to catch the ball a few times. Explain the importance of giving no indication that the one person is being left out on purpose.

- Have the volunteer return to the room.

- Start the game. Stop the game after every student who remained in the room has caught the ball at least three times.

- Ask the students how they enjoyed the game. If the student who was left out does not respond, ask directly how he/she liked the game. Be sure to draw out the fact that the student was left out and how he/she felt about what happened.

- Tell the students that one of the most important parts of self-understanding is the knowledge that everyone feels the need to belong and that this need to belong sometimes shows itself through different physical reactions.

- Explain that one reaction can be feeling irritable. Have the students describe times when they felt irritable because they were not included in a game or social function they wanted to be part of.

- Explain that another reaction can be the feeling of being uncomfortable. Then ask the students to name a time when they were uncomfortable about going into a new or different situation.

- Conclude the session by reviewing the fact that everyone has the basic need to belong and that this need is sometimes shown through different physical reactions. Have the students observe themselves and others between now and their next meeting to see if they can identify reactions associated with a need to belong.

BODY LANGUAGE AND NON-VERBAL COMMUNICATION

Objective:

To help students learn about the effects of body language and non-verbal communication and become aware that people often say one thing but their body language signals that they really mean something else

Materials Needed:

For each student:
☐ None

For the leader:
☑ Chart paper and marker
☑ Paper and red marker

Session Preparation:

Write the words *Science Test* as a heading on the piece of paper. Then, using the red marker, write a large letter "F" on the paper. Gather any other necessary materials.

Session:

• Begin the session by asking the students to share their observations of various physical reactions to wanting to belong. Especially note the students' observations about themselves.

• Write *Body Language* and *Non-Verbal Communication* on the chart paper. Then pantomime various feelings using body language and non-verbal communication. Some suggested feelings you should demonstrate are jealousy, fear, elation, anxiety, boredom, pride, sadness, depression, and worry. Include any others you wish.

• As you demonstrate each emotion, ask the students to identify the emotion and tell what led to their conclusion. Their answers will introduce the topics of *body language* and *non-verbal communication*. Record each student's answer on the chart, then put a checkmark after *Body Language*, *Non-Verbal Communication*, or both. Save this chart for the next session.

• Ask the students to demonstrate other emotions, using body language and non-verbal communication.

• Discuss how it is helpful to be able to identify and understand other people's emotions without having them actually tell what they are feeling.

• Direct the discussion to the topic of people saying one thing but meaning something completely different. Using body language, demonstrate how someone might look in such a situation. For example, hold up the *Science Test* paper with a large red "F" written across it and say, "It was a dumb test. It doesn't matter anyway."

• Involve the students in examples and demonstrations of people saying one thing, but meaning another. (***Note:*** Do not restrict the examples to children. Include parents and teachers as well.) After each example, ask the contributing student if the example was something he/she has done, something seen done by other people, or something made up.

• Conclude the session by asking the students to observe themselves and others for examples of body language and non-verbal communication and for people saying one thing but meaning another.

Objective:

To help the students understand that the behaviors and reactions learned in Sessions 1 and 2 affect human relationships

Materials Needed:

For each student:
☐ None

For the leader:
☑ *Body Language/Non-Verbal Communication* chart from Session 2

Session Preparation:

Gather the necessary materials.

Session:

• Review the topics presented in Sessions 1 and 2 by having the students discuss the issues of wanting to belong, non-verbal communication, and saying one thing but meaning another. Have the students give personal examples of these issues, showing that they have learned how each issue relates to them.

• Point to the emotions listed on the *Body Language/Non-Verbal Communication* chart. Review each emotion and ask the students how they deal with people they realize are feeling these emotions. Ask which category is most difficult to deal with.

• Reverse the strategy by having the students tell how different people deal with them when they are experiencing these emotions.

• Ask the students to define *Human Relationships*. After hearing a few responses, explain that what the group has been doing for the past three sessions is related to *Human Relationships*. Explain that this is because they have been learning about their reactions and the reactions of others when they interact with them.

• Have the students name *Human Relationships* at school and at home. (Some examples for school could be: getting along with classmates, caring about someone who is not having a good day, etc. For home: getting along with parents and siblings, giving extra help when someone needs it, etc.)

• Conclude the session by having the students complete the following sentences aloud:

> One thing I have learned about myself and wanting to belong at home is …

> One thing I have learned about myself and wanting to belong at school is …

> When I notice someone behaving in a manner that shows he or she wants to belong, I can …

> One thing I learned about the way I use body language at home is …

> One thing I learned about the way I use body language at school is …

> I can interpret someone's body language at school or at home by …

> One thing I have learned about myself and saying one thing and meaning another both at home and at school is …

Session 4
HELPING OTHERS AND BEING HELPED

Objective:

To have students experience the feelings generated when helping others and being helped by others

Materials Needed:

For each student:
- ☐ None

For the leader:
- ☑ Magazines and/or newspapers
- ☑ Scissors
- ☑ Construction paper
- ☑ Marker
- ☑ Tape

Session Preparation:

Cut several articles or pictures from newspapers or magazines describing or illustrating a person involved in a situation requiring the help of another person(s). The situations could be about divorce, death, drugs, violence, natural disaster, or any other situation you deem appropriate for your age group.

Do not use the headlines from the newspapers or magazines. Tape each article/picture onto construction paper, then write your own headline above the article/picture. Tape each article to the chalkboard/wall.

Session:

- Ask the students to look at the articles taped to the wall and think about how they would feel if they were involved in a situation of that kind.

- Then ask the following questions pertaining to each situation:

  If you were faced with this situation, how might you feel?

  How would the situation affect you at home?

  How would the situation affect you at school?

  How would the situation affect you with friends?

  What do you think a friend could do to help?

- Divide the students into pairs. Tell them they are going to role-play the situations taped to the wall. One person should play the person having the problem. The other should be a friend who might help.

- Have the students role-play as many situations as time permits. Have them switch roles so that each person has an opportunity to play both parts. (***Note:*** The role-plays may be done one at a time in front of the group or the partners may work on their own.)

- When the students have finished role-playing, ask how they felt being helped and how they felt when they were the helper.

- Conclude the session by asking the students what they learned about themselves. Have them complete the following sentences aloud:

  I learned that when I helped someone else, I felt …

  I learned that when someone helped me, I felt …

GROUPS TO GO: SMALL GROUPS FOR COUNSELORS ON THE GO © 2006 MAR∗CO PRODUCTS, INC. 1-800-448-2197

VISUALIZING HUMAN RELATIONSHIPS

Objective:

To have the students review the concepts taught and begin to incorporate them in a mural

Materials Needed:

For each student:
☐ None

For the leader:
☑ Brown mural paper
☑ Crayons or markers

Session Preparation:

Gather the necessary materials.

Session:

- Have the students briefly review what they have learned about a person's need to belong, emotions, ways of communicating non-verbally, and not saying what they really mean.

- Have the students tell what they learned about themselves in relation to these topics and what they need to do differently.

- Distribute brown mural paper and crayons or markers to the students. Tell the students they are going to make a mural that depicts the meaning of this group. It will be titled *Self-Understanding Improves Human Relationships*.

- Have the students discuss what topics their mural should include. *(Note:* Be sure they include that people want to belong, they do not want to be left out; they experience many different emotions, some positive, some negative, and some neutral; they communicate non-verbally through body language; and they should say what they mean, not what they think someone wants them to say.) Tell the students they should divide into teams and that each team should develop a particular topic.

- Conclude the session by having the teams decide how they will depict their topic so the mural shows that if people understand themselves in relation to these topics, they will have better relationships at school and at home. They may start on their mural if time allows.

SUMMARY

Objective:

To summarize the concepts taught in the previous sessions

Materials Needed:

For each student:
   ☐ None

For the leader:
   ☑ Mural begun in Session 5
   ☑ Crayons or markers
   ☑ Tape

Session Preparation:

Gather any necessary materials.

Session:

- Have the students complete their mural.

- Have each team explain the concept it was depicting and how it affects human relationships.

- Have the students tape the mural in an appropriate place in the hallway.

- Conclude the session by thanking the students for their participation and telling them that by understanding what was taught in these sessions and applying these concepts to their own lives, they will have greater self-confidence in their relationships with other people. That, in turn, will give them greater self-confidence to do the things in life that they choose to do.

179

SOCIAL SKILLS

Everyday Social Skills

Friendship

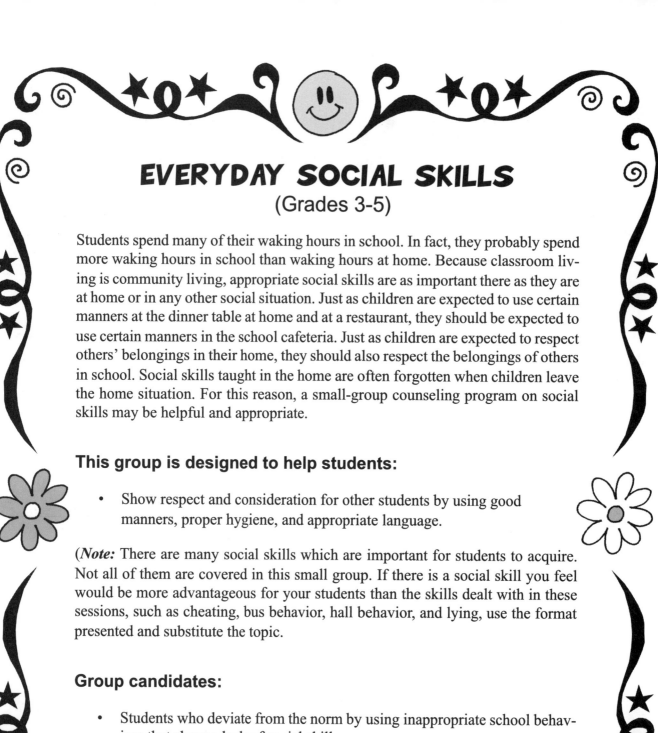

EVERYDAY SOCIAL SKILLS
(Grades 3-5)

Students spend many of their waking hours in school. In fact, they probably spend more waking hours in school than waking hours at home. Because classroom living is community living, appropriate social skills are as important there as they are at home or in any other social situation. Just as children are expected to use certain manners at the dinner table at home and at a restaurant, they should be expected to use certain manners in the school cafeteria. Just as children are expected to respect others' belongings in their home, they should also respect the belongings of others in school. Social skills taught in the home are often forgotten when children leave the home situation. For this reason, a small-group counseling program on social skills may be helpful and appropriate.

This group is designed to help students:

- Show respect and consideration for other students by using good manners, proper hygiene, and appropriate language.

(*Note:* There are many social skills which are important for students to acquire. Not all of them are covered in this small group. If there is a social skill you feel would be more advantageous for your students than the skills dealt with in these sessions, such as cheating, bus behavior, hall behavior, and lying, use the format presented and substitute the topic.

Group candidates:

- Students who deviate from the norm by using inappropriate school behaviors that show a lack of social skills
- Six to ten students from the same grade level

Group preparation:

Interview each student selected individually and explain the purpose and process of the group. Then send a parent notification and permission letter (page 183).

182

Dear _____,

Social skills are important for everyone. They are the key to peer acceptance. Without good social skills, children can be ostracized. They may spend precious time trying to make others notice and like them without having the skills to accomplish this task.

Your child's classroom teacher has identified your child as a student who could benefit from extra help in social skills.

In an effort to help your child and others learn more about this issue, I am forming a counseling group that will focus on helping children develop social skills they are called upon to use in everyday situations.

There will be six group meetings scheduled at a time the classroom teacher selects.

Your child knows about the group and has indicated that he or she would like to participate. However, no child is ever included in a small-group counseling program without his or her parents' knowledge and permission.

Please indicate, by completing the form below, that you wish to have your child participate in this group or that you do not want him or her to be included.

Return the permission slip to me by _____.

Thank you,

✂- -

☐ I, _____, *give permission* for my child to participate in the small-group counseling program for improving social skills.

☐ I, _____, *do not give permission* for my child to participate in the small-group counseling program for improving social skills.

Child's Name _____   Date _____

School _____   Grade _____

Teacher _____

Home Phone (____) _____   Work Phone (____) _____

Parent's Printed Name _____

Parent's Signature _____

DEFINING SOCIAL SKILLS

Objective:

To help children understand the meaning of *social skills*

Materials Needed:

For each student:
  ☐ None

For the leader:
  ☑ Chalkboard and chalk or chart paper and marker
  ☑ Construction paper for a poster
  ☑ Crayons or markers

Session Preparation:

Gather the necessary materials.

Session:

- Ask the students the following questions. Write their answers on the board/chart paper.

  What are some of the things your parents expect you to do when are at a dinner table?

  What are some of the things your parents expect you to do when you are at a restaurant?

  What are some of the things your parents expect you to do when you visit relatives?

- When the list is complete, select some of the answers and have the students explain the reasons for their answers. Bring out the point that parents' expectations make living with or being around other people more pleasant. Give the example that it is much more pleas-ant to talk with someone who does not have a mouthful of food than with one who is chewing and talking at the same time.

- When the students understand the concept of *good social skills*, divide them into pairs. Have the pairs work together to determine what would be good social skills to use at school. Then have the students share their answers with the group.

- Tell the students that during the next five sessions, they will be learning about appropriate social skills to use in school. Explain that one social skill will be discussed at each session and one pair of students will be responsible for presenting a poster illustrating acceptable social skills.

- Divide the students into five groups. If there is an uneven number of students, ask for volunteers to work on more then one presentation. Make sure there are at least two students in each group.

- Assign each group one of the following topics and tell them the presentation date:

      Cafeteria behavior
      Hygiene
      Inappropriate noises and language
      Respect for others' property
      Cliques and bullies

- Tell the students that they are responsible for making a poster about their topic and that their poster must be completed and ready for hanging on the wall the day of their presentation.

- Conclude the session by telling the students that in the next session, they will be discussing cafeteria behavior. Distribute construction paper and crayons or markers to the students responsible for making a poster about this topic.

CAFETERIA BEHAVIOR

Objective:

To discuss inappropriate cafeteria behaviors and make a contract for improvement

Materials Needed:

For each student:
- ☑ Copy of *Cafeteria Behavior Contract* (page 186)
- ☑ Pencil

For one student group:
- ☑ *Cafeteria Behavior* Poster

For the leader
- ☑ Chalkboard and chalk or chart paper and marker
- ☑ Construction paper for a poster
- ☑ Crayons or markers
- ☑ Tape

Session Preparation:

Reproduce *Cafeteria Behavior Contract* for each student. Gather any other necessary materials.

Session:

- Begin the session by collecting the crayons/markers that were given to the students responsible for making this session's poster. Have the assigned students present their poster on cafeteria behavior. Have the students who presented the poster tape it to the wall.

- Have the class name as many inappropriate cafeteria behaviors as possible. Record their answers on the board/chart paper.

- Have the students rank the answers from *bad* to *very worst*.

- The students should then tell what could be done to change the very worst behavior.

- Have the group brainstorm ideas on better social skills in the cafeteria.

- Distribute the *Cafeteria Behavior Contract* and a pencil to each student and assign each student a partner. Have the students complete the contracts, signing them and giving them to their partners.

- Explain that partners will be observing cafeteria behavior between now and the next session. The partner will then complete the contract according to what he/she has observed.

- Conclude the session by telling the students that the next session will be about hygiene. Distribute the construction paper and markers or crayons to the students who will be making the hygiene poster.

CAFETERIA BEHAVIOR CONTRACT

I will improve my cafeteria behavior by

_____

_____

_____

_____

My partner, _____ ,
will observe me and report my progress to the class.

Signed _____

I, _____ ,

felt that _____

fulfilled the contract.

I, _____ ,

felt that _____

did not fulfill the contract.

Objective:

To discuss the advantages of good hygiene and the disadvantages of poor hygiene

Materials Needed:

For each student group:
- ☑ Lined or unlined paper
- ☑ Pencil or markers

For one student group:
- ☑ *Hygiene* Poster

For the leader
- ☑ Construction paper for a poster
- ☑ Crayons or markers
- ☑ Tape

Session Preparation:

Gather the necessary materials.

Session:

- Begin the session by having the students report on their cafeteria observations. The completed contracts should be returned to the students being observed.

- Collect the crayons/markers that were given to the students responsible for making this session's poster. Introduce the topic of *hygiene* by having the assigned students present their poster. Have the students who presented the poster tape it to the wall.

- Divide the students into small groups. Assign each group one or more particular hygiene topic or topics. Suggested topics could include dental hygiene (cleaning teeth and gums); personal hygiene (bathing or showering, wearing clean clothes); health hygiene (washing hands, covering mouth when sneezing or coughing); etc. Tell each group to make a chart telling the advantages of good hygiene and the disadvantages of poor hygiene for each topic. The chart should also tell how often a person should perform each type of hygiene and the supplies needed to do so.

- Distribute a sheet of lined or unlined paper and a pencil or markers to each group. Tell the students how much time they have to complete the activity.

- When the allotted time has elapsed, have each group present its topic(s).

  (*Note:* The leader may choose to reproduce the charts on a copier for distribution to the students in the group.)

- Conclude the lesson by telling the group that the next session will be on inappropriate noises and language. Distribute the construction paper and markers or crayons to the students who will be making the inappropriate noises and language poster.

INAPPROPRIATE NOISES AND LANGUAGE

Objective:

To make the students aware of the reasons that students use inappropriate language or make inappropriate noises

Materials Needed:

For each student:
☐ None

For one student group:
☑ *Inappropriate Noises And Language* Poster

For the leader:
☑ Construction paper for a poster
☑ Crayons or markers
☑ Tape

Session Preparation:

Gather the necessary materials.

Session:

• Begin the session by collecting the crayons/markers that were given to the students responsible for making this session's poster. Have the assigned students present their poster on inappropriate noises and language. Have the students who presented the poster tape it on the wall.

• Explain to the students that this topic applies to noises made and words said intentionally as well as unintentionally and that there is a definite difference between the two. A noise such as laughing loudly, sneezing, burping, or expelling gas sometimes occurs without warning and the student to whom it happens is embarrassed. Inappropriate words are sometimes said in anger or haste before the student takes the time to think and the student is embarrassed. At other times, these noises are made and words are said because the student has poor social skills or because the student wants to attract attention. It is in these situations that the students need to know how to react. Whether the noises are made or words are said intentionally or unintentionally, ignoring the incident is the best way to stop the behavior.

• Discuss the following questions:

Why do students notice when someone uses inappropriate language or makes inappropriate noises?

Do you think the person making the inappropriate noises or using the inappropriate language is doing it so he or she will be noticed?

Why would a person want to be noticed?

What effect does an inappropriate noise have on other students? (Someone who intentionally burps loudly, for example, may embarrass the surrounding students who may feel others would think they burped or be angry because they were interrupted.)

What makes one word inappropriate and another appropriate?

Why are certain words and noises appropriate in some places but not in school?

• Conclude the session by telling the students that the next session will deal with respect for other people's property. Distribute the construction paper and markers or crayons to the students responsible for the poster on this topic.

Session 5
RESPECT FOR OTHER PEOPLE'S PROPERTY

Objective:

To have the students analyze ways people disrespect other people's property and come to conclusions about how these people will function in their community and as adults

Materials Needed:

For each student:
- ☐ None

For one student group:
- ☑ *Respect For Other People's Property* Poster

For the leader
- ☑ Chalkboard and chalk or chart paper and marker
- ☑ Construction paper for a poster
- ☑ Crayons or markers
- ☑ Tape

Session Preparation:

Gather the necessary materials.

Session:

- Begin the session by collecting the crayons/markers that were given to the students responsible for making this session's poster. Have the assigned students present their poster on respect for other people's property. Have the students who presented the poster tape it on the wall.

- Write the following words on the board/chart paper: *steal, destroy, deface.* Ask the students to give examples, using these words, in regard to disrespect for other people's property in school.

- Have the students tell how much of a problem this issue is in their classroom or school and why they believe these things happen.

- Discuss the following questions:

  Is it ever appropriate to steal, destroy, or deface someone else's property? (**Note:** This question will undoubtedly lead into the issue of "getting back" at someone and whether that is appropriate behavior. The leader must be aware of the students' environment outside of the school system and deal with this question accordingly.)

  What are the feelings of the person who is not respectful of other people's property?

  What are the feelings of the person whose property is not respected?

  If students are not respectful of other people's property in school, what do you think could happen to these same people when they go into the community and become adults?

- Conclude the session by telling the students that the next session will deal with cliques and bullies. Distribute the construction paper and markers or crayons to the students responsible for the poster on this topic.

Objective:

To identify the behaviors found in cliques and bullies and relate them to social issues in our country and the world

Materials Needed:

For each student group:
- ☑ Pencil

For one student group:
- ☑ *Cliques And Bullies* poster

For the leader:
- ☑ 2 pieces of paper
- ☑ Marker
- ☑ Tape

Session Preparation:

Title one piece of paper: *In order to be in a clique, I have to …*

Title the other piece of paper: *In order to be a bully, I have to …*

Gather any other necessary materials.

Session:

- Begin the session by collecting the crayons/markers that were given to the students responsible for making this session's poster. Have the assigned students present their poster on cliques and bullies. Have the students who presented the poster tape it to the wall.

- Explain to the students that almost everyone wants friends. In most cases, the person who loudly proclaims he/she doesn't have or want any friends really wants friends very badly.

- Divide the students into two groups. Label one group *Bullies* and the other *Cliques*.

- Give each group the piece of paper that corresponds to its group assignment and a pencil. Have the group members complete the sentence at the top of the paper by listing as many characteristics as they can.

- Then ask one student from each group to read its list aloud.

- Have the students discuss why they believe some students are bullies and why cliques are so popular.

- Briefly discuss the following questions:

   How do bullies behave?

   How can students react to a bully in ways that will help change the bully's behavior?

- The issue of being in a clique may be difficult to discuss because in many classrooms, the most popular students form cliques and the idea of discussing anything negative about these students is unpopular. So ask the following questions:

   How is someone invited to join or accepted into a clique?

   Are some people never invited to join or accepted into a clique? Why do you think this is so?

- Once it is known that some people are ostracized for whatever reasons, ask the students to tell how the cliques they are talking about differ from certain ethnic groups being treated unfairly. If appropriate, mention the plight of women in some Third World countries, the Jews in Germany during World War II, the African-Americans during their fight for equal rights, women in the United States not being able to vote in the early 1900s, etc. Before closing this topic, make sure the students understand that the examples given and cliques both stem from the same basic concept.

- Conclude the group by having the students complete the following sentences aloud:

   One thing I learned about cafeteria behavior is …

   One thing I learned about hygiene is …

   One thing I learned about inappropriate noises and language is …

   One thing I learned about respecting other people's property is …

   One thing I learned about cliques and bullies is …

   I know that good social skills are important because …

191

FRIENDSHIP
(Grades 4-5)

Peer relationships are an important part of a student's life. As students grow older, the pull to peers becomes stronger. This desire to belong affects a student's academic performance, self-worth, and overall behavior.

This group is designed to help students:

- Better understand themselves in relation to their peers
- Recognize what they like and admire in peers
- Learn what it means to be a friend
- Find ways to improve their friendship skills

Group candidates:

- Students who have difficulty making friends
- Students who have or show the possibility of making friends with students who have behavior difficulties
- Six to eight students from the same grade level

Group preparation:

Interview each student selected individually and explain the purpose and process of the group. Then send a parent notification and permission letter (page 193).

Dear _____,

Peer relationships are important for everyone. They affect a student's academic performance, behaviors, and sense of self-worth. Good peer relationships are developed through good friendship skills.

Your child's classroom teacher has identified your child as a student who could benefit from extra help in developing friendship skills.

In an effort to help your child and others learn more about this issue, I am forming a counseling group that will focus on helping children to understand themselves and what they need to do to form positive friendships.

There will be six group meetings scheduled at a time the classroom teacher selects.

Your child knows about the group and has indicated that he or she would like to participate. However, no child is ever included in a small-group counseling program without his or her parents' knowledge and permission.

Please indicate, by completing the form below, that you wish to have your child participate in this group or that you do not want him or her to be included.

Return the permission slip to me by _____.

Thank you,

✂ -

☐ I, _____, *give permission* for my child to participate in the small-group counseling program for developing friendship skills.

☐ I, _____, *do not give permission* for my child to participate in the small-group counseling program for developing friendship skills.

Child's Name _____   Date _____

School _____   Grade _____

Teacher _____

Home Phone (____) _____   Work Phone (____) _____

Parent's Printed Name _____

Parent's Signature _____

Session 1
LEARNING ABOUT MYSELF

Objective:

To have the students construct a "picture" of their social interactions

Materials Needed:

For each student:
- ☑ Paper
- ☑ Pencil

For the leader:
- ☐ None

Session Preparation:

Gather the necessary materials.

Session:

- Tell the students they will be meeting six times to learn how to be a good friend.

- The leader should take 90 seconds to tell the children something he/she likes about him/herself. Then have the students introduce themselves by giving each student 90 seconds to say anything he/she likes about him/herself.

- Distribute paper and a pencil to each student. Have the students put their names on their papers. Tell the students that before they can have good friendship skills, they need to know the things they themselves like to do.

- Give the group five minutes to list as many things as they can think of that they like to do. It can be something they do often or something they have only done once. It can be something they have done at home, in school, at play, on a vacation, or at any time. But it must be something they have done, not something they would like to do.

- When the allotted time has elapsed, have the students identify how often they do each thing. They may do this by putting a + by something they do frequently and a – by something they do infrequently. Have the students tally the number of +'s and –'s, write that number at the bottom of their paper, and share their numbers with the group.

- When the students have finished, have them look at their list again and put an F next to everything they do with their family, a C next to everything they do with classmates/friends, and an A next to everything they do alone. Have the students tally the number of F's, C's, and A's, write that number at the bottom of their paper, and share their numbers with the group.

- Tell the students that the paper they have before them is like a picture of what they like to do and with whom they like doing these things.

- Conclude the session by having each student write at the bottom of his/her paper a statement that begins, "Today I learned that _____." Allow each student who wishes to share his/her statement.

- Collect the papers and save them for the next session.

194

PEOPLE WHO INFLUENCE ME

Objective:

To make the students become aware of people who influence them

Materials Needed:

For each student:
- ☑ List from Session 1
- ☑ Piece of paper
- ☑ Piece of graph paper
- ☑ Pencil

For the leader:
- ☑ Chalkboard and chalk or chart paper and marker

Session Preparation:

Gather the necessary materials.

Session:

- Return the lists collected in Session 1. Ask the students to look them over.

- Distribute paper, a pencil, and graph paper to each student. Have the students put their names on both the paper and graph paper.

- Tell the students, based on what they wrote on the list in Session 1, to name 5-10 people they believe influence them. They should write these names on their paper, then rank them with "1" being the most influential to whatever number of names they have listed. The highest number should be the least influential.

- Draw a rectangle on the board/chart paper and add squares like a bar graph. Then ask the students to suggest five names of people who influence them. Write those names on the board/chart paper. Have the students select the name of the person from the board/chart paper who would influence them most. Draw a bar graph from the bottom of the paper to the point that shows how much influence that person has. Label it with that name. Continue doing this with the other four names.

- Have the students title the graph paper *Who Influences Me And How Much*. Then tell the students to use the bar graph on the board/chart paper as a guide and make their own bar graph showing who influences them and how much influence each person has on them.

- Have the students share their finished papers. As the students identify the choices written on their graphs, write only the category (such as teacher), not the person's name on the chalkboard/chartpaper. Tally the final results.

- Using this information, discuss:

  The number of similar people who influence each of them.

  The uniqueness or lack of uniqueness of each bar graph.

  How influential people may change their lives.

- Conclude the lesson by collecting the paper from the first session and the papers from this session. Save the papers for the final session when they will be compiled into a booklet.

GROUPS TO GO: SMALL GROUPS FOR COUNSELORS ON THE GO © 2006 MAR*CO PRODUCTS, INC. 1-800-448-2197

Session 3
WHAT I LIKE ABOUT OTHER PEOPLE

Objective:

To have the students examine the characteristics of the people they like

Materials Needed:

For each student:
- ☑ Old magazine
- ☑ 12" x 18" construction paper
- ☑ Gluestick
- ☑ Scissors

For the leader:
- ☑ Paper
- ☑ Pencil

Session Preparation:

Gather the necessary materials.

Session:

- Distribute the construction paper, one magazine, a gluestick, and scissors to each student.

- Explain that the students' task for this session is to make a collage. They should go through their magazine and cut out any words or pictures that will show or tell things they like in another person. They should then glue what they have cut out onto the construction paper to form a collage.

- Allow ample time for the students to do this project. About 10 minutes before the session is to end, have the students share their collages with the group.

- As the students are sharing their collages, list the words they have selected and make copies for the students to use in Session 4.

- Ask the students if they believe the words and pictures they have chosen are traits that others would look for in a friend.

- Conclude the lesson by telling the students that the words and pictures they have chosen are a "picture" of an ideal friend.

- Collect the collages.

GROUPS TO GO: SMALL GROUPS FOR COUNSELORS ON THE GO © 2006 MAR*CO PRODUCTS, INC. 1-800-448-2197

STRENGTHS AND WANNABES

Objective:

To have the students identify the strengths they possess and strengths they would like to possess

Materials Needed:

For each student:
- ☑ List from Session 3
- ☑ Copy of *Strengths And Wannabes* (page 198)
- ☑ Pencil

For the leader:
- ☑ List from Session 3

Session Preparation:

Reproduce the word list from Session 3 and *Strengths And Wannabes* for each student. Gather any other necessary materials.

Session:

- Distribute the list of words from Session 3 and a pencil to each student. Tell the students this is a list of characteristics they said they admired in others. Have the students circle each characteristic they believe they have and put an "X" after each uncircled characteristic they would like to have.

- Distribute *Strengths And Wannabes* to each student. Have the students put their names and the date on the sheet. Tell the students to use the list from Session 3 and select the five strongest traits they have that they feel would help them to be a good friend and write those choices on the activity sheet. When everyone has finished, have each student select one choice and tell the group why that trait was included on his/her activity sheet.

- Tell the students to use the list of words from Session 3 and look carefully at those traits after which they placed an "X." These are traits that they do not have but would like to have. Have them write three of these traits on the activity sheet.

- Discuss, with the students, how someone can acquire a trait he/she would like to have. Look at the list from Session 3 and select one trait. The trait need not be one a student has selected. Have the students suggest how someone who did not have this trait could acquire it.

- Have the students complete the activity sheet by identifying ways they could change their wannabes into strengths.

- Allow those students who wish to do so to share what they have written.

- Collect the activity sheets.

Name_____   Date_____

STRENGTHS AND WANNABES

★ **Strengths I have are:**

   1. _____
   2. _____
   3. _____
   4. _____
   5. _____

★ **Strengths I would like to have are:**

   1. _____
   2. _____
   3. _____

★ **Ways I can make my wannabes into strengths are:**

   1. _____
      _____
   2. _____
      _____
   3. _____
      _____

198

Objective:

To help the students understand how to be a friend and how to make friends

Materials Needed:

For each student:
- ☑ Copy of *Being A Friend And Making Friends* (page 200)
- ☑ Pencil

For the leader:
- ☑ Chalkboard and chalk or chart paper and marker

Session Preparation:

Reproduce *Being A Friend And Making Friends* for each student. Gather any other necessary materials.

Session:

- Write the word *FRIENDSHIP* in large letters vertically on the board/chart paper. Ask the students to tell you how someone acts if he/she is in a friendship. Tell them to think of things that begin with the letters in *friendship*. Write the students' suggestions on the board/chart paper. For example:

F	Finds things to do that we both like
R	Really listens when I talk
I	Is interesting
E	Explains things I don't understand
N	Never talks behind my back
D	Doesn't lie to me
S	Suggests things we can do together
H	Helps me when I need help
I	Includes others when we do things together
P	Plays fairly

- Give the students an opportunity to describe other ways friends behave. Add their suggestions to the *FRIENDSHIP* list. The leader may make suggestions as well.

- Distribute *Being A Friend And Making Friends* and a pencil to each student. Tell the students to put their names and the date on their papers, then look at the top of their activity sheet. Then, using suggestions from the board/chart paper or any of their own, write three ways they can be a friend.

- On the board/chart paper, write *MAKE FRIENDS* in a vertical line. Then ask the students to do the same thing with these words as they did with *friendship,* but this time, tell them to name things they can do to make new friends. Examples would be:

M	Make sure you listen to what the person is saying
A	Ask the person's name
K	Keep trying if it doesn't work out the first time
E	Eat lunch with the person
F	Find out what the person likes to do
R	Respect what the person has to say
I	Introduce yourself
E	Express your desire to know the person better
N	Name some things you like to do
D	Don't do all the talking
S	Share something that you have

- Have the students complete the bottom half of their activity sheet by selecting ideas from the board/chart paper or using some of their own.

- Have each student share one thing from the top half of the activity sheet and one thing from the bottom half of the activity sheet.

- Conclude the session by encouraging the students to make one new friend this week using the ideas they selected to put on their lists. Collect the students' papers.

Name_____   Date_____

BEING A FRIEND AND MAKING FRIENDS

★ **Some ways I can be a friend are:**

1. _____
   _____

2. _____
   _____

3. _____
   _____

★ **Some ways I can make a new friend are:**

1. _____
   _____

2. _____
   _____

3. _____
   _____

Objective:

To have the students review what they have learned about friendship

Materials Needed:

For each student:
- ☑ 10 3" x 5" index cards
- ☑ Black crayon or marker

For the leader:
- ☑ Students' papers from previous sessions
- ☑ Friendship word list
- ☑ Stapler and staples
- ☑ 3" x 5" index cards
- ☑ Chalkboard and chalk or chart paper and marker (optional)

Session Preparation:

Make a list of about 10 character-trait words associated with being a good friend. Suggestions are: *Kind, Nice, Helpful, Honest, Shares, Takes Turns, Listens, Caring, Respectful, Trustworthy.* Gather any other necessary materials.

Session:

- Begin the session by asking the students to share the experiences they had when making a new friend.

- Distribute 10 3" x 5" index cards and a black crayon or marker to each student. Tell the students to pick any 10 letters of the alphabet. They may choose different letters or the same letters. Have them write one letter on each card.

- Explain that they will now play a game. You will read a list of character traits that good friends have. (*Note:* If spelling may be a problem, write the words on the board/chart paper.) Read one word at a time. When you read the first word, ask the students to raise their hands if the first letter of the word is one they have on their cards. Select one student who will come to the front of the room and hold up his/her index card printed with that letter. That student will then say the second letter of the word you read. Students having that letter on their card will raise their hands. The student will select one of those students to come to the front of the room. Each time a letter is needed, the last student to come to the front of the room will pick the next person. This will continue until the word is completely spelled. (*Note:* If no student has a needed letter write the letter on one of the extra cards and let a student hold two letters.)

- Return all the previously collected papers to the students. Tell them to fold their collages in half. They will use these as their cover. Have them use their marker or crayon to write the words FRIENDSHIP on the cover and place their papers inside it. Staple each booklet together.

- Conclude the group by thanking the students for their participation and encourage them to use the papers in their booklets to remind them of what they learned and to continue to make new friends as well as keep the ones they already have.

TEST-TAKING

Controlling Test-Taking Feelings

Test-Taking Techniques

CONTROLLING TEST-TAKING FEELINGS
(Grades 3-5)

The word *test* conjures up all sorts of feelings. Some students become nervous, others are frightened, and some get stomachaches. Almost nobody looks forward to a test. The negative feelings that students have can affect their performance if the feelings take control of them. Anxiety can cause a student not to think clearly, remember known facts, or write answers carefully. Since tests are an important part of the educational system and students' reactions to them affects their performance, providing a small-group counseling program can help these students deal with their feelings.

The purpose of this small group is not only to have the students identify their feelings and their causes. Its strength also lies in the fact that each group member participates in helping the others overcome their anxieties. This occurs in the second half of the group sessions. In the first half of the group sessions, the groundwork is laid for understanding the causes of anxiety. The second half of the group sessions involves the students giving each other suggestions to reduce test anxiety and each group member making a commitment to implement one of the suggestions during the time period between the sessions.

This group is designed to help students:

- Identify their feelings about taking tests and the causes of these feelings
- Learn techniques for overcoming their feelings about taking tests

Group candidates:

- Students who do well in classwork but have difficulty with testing situations (*Note:* Students who do not do well with classwork should not be considered for this group. It is impossible to tell how these students are affected by testing situations, because they do not try to do their daily work.)
- Only students who wish to participate should be included in the group
- Six to eight students from the same grade level

Group preparation:

Interview each student selected individually and explain the purpose and process of the group. Then send a parent notification and permission letter (page 205). Ask the students' teachers to give you a list of the test grades earned by each student in each subject for the last marking period, any test grades for the present marking period, and the students most recent report card grades.

Dear _____,

Test-taking is an important part not only of the educational system, but also of life. Throughout life, we will be asked to take tests for one thing or another. Many will be job-related and will determine whether we are hired or promoted to a better position.

Students who do well in their classwork but "freeze up" when it comes to taking a teacher-made or standardized test suffer from anxiety, feelings of failure, and lack of confidence in themselves. Your child's classroom teacher has identified your child as one of these students.

In an effort to help your child and others learn more about this issue, I am forming a counseling group that will focus on helping children control their test-taking anxiety. They will explore the cause of their feelings and learn strategies for overcoming these fears.

There will be six group meetings scheduled at a time the classroom teacher selects.

Your child knows about the group and has indicated that he or she would like to participate. However, no child is ever included in a small-group counseling program without his or her parents' knowledge and permission.

Please indicate, by completing the form below, that you wish to have your child participate in this group or that you do not want him or her to be included.

Return the permission slip to me by _____.

Thank you,

✂ -

☐ I, _____, *give permission* for my child to participate in the small-group counseling program to reduce text anxiety.

☐ I, _____, *do not give permission* for my child to
participate in the small-group counseling program to reduce text anxiety.

Child's Name _____   Date _____

School _____   Grade _____

Teacher _____

Home Phone (____) _____   Work Phone (____) _____

Parent's Printed Name _____

Parent's Signature _____

205

WHY TESTS?

Objective:

To examine the pros and cons of having tests

Materials Needed:

For each student:
- ☐ None

For the leader:
- ☑ Copy of each student's test scores
- ☑ Chalkboard and chalk or chart paper and marker

Session Preparation:

Gather the necessary materials.

Session:

- Begin by explaining that the purpose of the group is to help the students deal more effectively with the entire test-taking process. Then review some basic rules of confidentiality and behavior.

- Distribute a copy of the test grades given to you by the teacher to the students to whom they belong. Have the students look them over, but do not comment on the tests at this time. Collect the test scores and save them for use in the next session.

- Write the letters *TEST* vertically on the chalkboard/chart paper. Then ask the students to make up four sentences about how they feel about taking tests. Each sentence should begin with one of the letters in *TEST*.

For example:

- **T** aking a test ruins my whole day.
- **E** ven if I know the answers, I can't concentrate long enough to write them down.
- **S** tudying for a test does me no good.
- **T** rying my best only makes me do my worst.

If the number of students in the group is a multiple of four, do the exercise as many times as necessary to allow each student to make up a sentence. If the number of students in the group is not a multiple of four, repeat the letters from the word as needed. For example, for a group of six you could use T-E-S-T-T-E.

- Divide the students into two groups. Tell the students that they are going to have a debate. One group will argue that tests are necessary. The other will argue that tests are not necessary. Give the students time to prepare their presentations.

- Give each group uninterrupted time to present its case. Allow enough time for questions to be directed to both sides. Be sure to enforce the rule of *no interrupting while someone is talking*.

- About five minutes before the session ends, stop the debate and sum up what you have heard. Tell the group that even though they do not have the power to decide whether to eliminate tests, it is good to think about both sides of the issue. Identify any feelings that were evident about testing. Remember what was has been expressed for review in Session 2.

- Conclude the session by saying that in the next session, the students will begin to explore the different reasons for feeling the way they do in a testing situation.

WHAT CAUSES THE FEELINGS ASSOCIATED WITH TEST-TAKING?

Objective:

To identify different feelings associated with test-taking

Materials Needed:

For each student:
- ☐ None

For the leader:
- ☑ Copy of each student's test scores
- ☑ Paper or note cards
- ☑ Pencil

Session Preparation:

Gather the necessary materials.

Session:

- Begin the session by reviewing the feelings about tests expressed in Session 1.

- Ask the students to answer the following questions:

   What goes through your mind when the teacher announces a test date?

   What is it like at home the night before a test?

   What is it like during the school day before a test is given?

   How do you feel during a test?

   When a test is over, how do you feel?

Allow each student to answer each question before asking the next one. On a piece of paper or note cards, jot down significant feelings expressed by each student. Review at least one feeling for each student by asking questions in the following way:

Kirk, you said you feel like throwing up when you hear the teacher say there will be a social studies test on Friday. What is it about a test that makes you feel sick?

Jerry, you said you had a hard time getting to sleep the night before a test because you were hyper. What is it about a test that makes you be hyper?

Cindy, you said that as the test time gets closer in the school day, you get more and more nervous. What is it about a test that makes you nervous?

Bonnie, you said that you feel mixed up while you're taking a test. What is it about a test that makes you feel mixed up?

Pete, you said that once the test is over, you feel worried. What is it about a test that makes you feel worried?

- Tell the students that when they allow their feelings to control their actions, they do not function as effectively as they can.

- Give each student his/her test scores and ask them to look at the grades. Explain that until they gain control of their feelings, they will have difficulty when faced with a testing situation. Collect the test scores and save them for use in Session 6.

- Conclude the session by telling the students that the next two sessions will explore ways to control of their feelings.

Session 3
FINDING THE CAUSE

Objective:

To help each student deal with the reasons for his/her feelings associated with a testing situation

Materials Needed:

For each student:
☐ None

For the leader:
☑ Notes taken at the last session

Session Preparation:

Gather the necessary materials.

Session:

* Begin the session by reviewing the different feelings about tests you heard expressed in the previous sessions.

* Since the students' reasons will be very different, the following are only sample suggestions that might be used. Address one student at a time, using the information learned in the last lesson in the following manner:

    Kirk, last week you said that when you hear you are going to have a test, you feel like throwing up. You thought that the reason for this sick feeling was that the thought of having to take a test made your stomach do flip-flops.

Jerry, last week you said that the night before a test you could hardly sleep because you were so hyper. You said that the reason you were hyper was because you couldn't get the next day's test out of your mind. The more you tried to sleep, the more you mentally kept trying to answer questions. Your mind just wouldn't shut off.

Cindy, last week you said that during the school day, you got more and more nervous as the time to take the test got closer. You said you thought the reason was that you were worried about what questions the teacher was going to ask and whether you had studied the right things.

Bonnie, last week you said you felt mixed up when you took a test. You thought the reason was that when you read a question a whole lot of answers came into your head. Pretty soon, you just got all mixed up and couldn't figure out which one was right.

Pete, last week you said that after a test was over, you felt worried. The reason for this feeling was that you felt you might disappoint your parents and be embarrassed in front of your friends.

- Introduce the concept of contributions from each group member by telling the students that each of them is to think of something their fellow group members could do that might help relieve their anxieties. Explain that after each group member has made a contribution, the group member to whom the suggestions were directed must select one suggestion to use between this session and the next session. Begin by reviewing the information reviewed at the beginning of this lesson. Then have the other group members suggest how each student could solve his/her problem. Examples of suggestions might be:

Kirk, when you hear there is going to be a test, you could immediately think of something you enjoy doing and pretend you are doing it right that minute. Get the test off your mind and something else on it. But remember that you're in class, so you cannot daydream for too long.

Jerry, you need to learn to shut your mind off to test questions. Pick a super-dull book, one you really don't want to read. Start reading it until you can't keep your eyes open any longer. Then quickly shut off the light and go to sleep.

Cindy, every time you think about the test during the school day, immediately tell yourself that you studied the right things. Say this to yourself five times, then get back to what you were doing.

Bonnie, when you get mixed up and everything seems jumbled, sit back and read the question again. Then slowly think of how you will answer the question. If it is an essay question, write each sentence as you think of it. If it is another type of question, look at the possible answers and slowly eliminate the ones that you believe are not correct.

Pete, talk with your parents about how you feel about possibly disappointing them. If your friends tease you about grades, maybe you'd better decide if these guys are really friends.

When all the students who wish to have given suggestions, the leader may add possible solutions.

- When all of the students have had an opportunity to hear the suggestions, ask each student which suggestion he/she would be willing to try. They must choose one. Tell them they are to use the solution that they chose and report on it at the next session.

- Conclude this session with, "If there's a test this week, what are you going to do, (NAME)?" Have the students give their answers.

Objective:

To allow students to review the chosen solutions and learn to talk about feelings with parents and friends

Materials Needed:

For each student:
☐ None

For the leader:
☐ None

Session Preparation:

None.

Session:

• Begin the session with a report from the students about how their chosen technique for conquering test anxiety worked. If the chosen solution was successful, the student should continue to use it. If it was not successful, the group must offer additional solutions and the student must make another choice. (**Note:** This process will take place in the final three sessions. By allotting three sessions to finding a successful solution, the counselor is not rushed and students may experiment with different solutions. The student who has immediate success takes on a consulting role and continues to play an important part in the group.)

• Introduce the solution of talking with parents and friends about feelings of worry and embarrassment. This is a good technique to have the students learn because it is a technique every student in the group should know and use.

• Present the technique as a role-play activity. Select one student to present his/her feelings to other members of the group. Designate some of the students to take on the role of parents and others to take on the role of peers. Tell them to enact the situations as realistically as possible. Give every student an opportunity to be the student with a concern.

• Discuss the process and remind the students that they are to talk about their feelings of worry and embarrassment with both their parents and/or a friend before the next session. They are also to use their chosen technique for conquering test anxiety.

VISUALIZING A PLEASANT SITUATION

Objective:

To allow students to review the chosen solutions and learn to get rid of an unpleasant situation by visualizing a pleasant situation.

Materials Needed:

For each student:
 ☐ None

For the leader:
 ☐ None

Session Preparation:

None.

Session:

• Begin the session by getting each student's reaction to his/her chosen technique and to talking with his/her parents and/or friends. If the chosen solution was successful, the student should continue to use it. If it was not successful, the group must offer additional solutions and the student must make another choice.

• Introduce the solution of getting rid of an unpleasant situation by visualizing a pleasant situation. This is another technique that can be useful in many situations, including test-taking.

• Have each student select several pleasant situations. Have the students concentrate, with their eyes open, on their chosen situations. Then have each student finish the sentence, "Tomorrow is the chapter test in math and I wish _____." Discuss the endings deliberately trying to the upset students. When the discussion looks as if it is producing unhealthy feelings, tell the students to mentally go to their pleasant situations. Give the students three minutes to stay in their pleasant situations, then call them back together.

• Discuss the activity. Emphasize that mentally divorcing themselves from an unpleasant situation is difficult, because they have to do it without calling attention to themselves and they have to bring themselves back within an appropriate time limit. Practice the exercise a few more times, using different sentences.

• Tell the students to continue using their chosen text-anxiety technique and practice the new technique of visualizing pleasant situations whenever they feel themselves becoming overly anxious. Remind them that nobody must know they are using the technique. It must be done with their eyes open and as inconspicuously as possible.

GROUPS TO GO: SMALL GROUPS FOR COUNSELORS ON THE GO © 2006 MAR★CO PRODUCTS, INC. 1-800-448-2197

Session 6
TRAINING YOUR MIND TO ORGANIZE THOUGHTS EFFECTIVELY

Objective:

To review the chosen anxiety-reducing solutions and learn to organize thoughts effectively

Materials Needed:

For each student:
☐ None

For the leader:
☑ Copy of each student's test scores
☑ All test scores for each student that have occurred since the first group session
☑ Material being studied at present in the students' classrooms

Session Preparation:

Obtain all test scores since the first session from the students' teachers. Ask the students' teachers for some material that they are studying at the present time.

Session:

- Begin the session by eliciting each student's reaction to his/her chosen suggestion and to visualizing a pleasant situation to get rid of an unpleasant situation. If the chosen solution was successful, the student should continue to use it. If it was not successful, the group must offer additional solutions and the student must make another choice.

- Introduce the solution of *training the mind to organize thoughts effectively*. This is another technique that can be useful for all students in many situations, including test-taking.

- Using the material provided by the teachers, give the students examples for them to use to practice organizing their thoughts. These could include math problems to be worked, a topic in social studies that might be an essay question, or a spelling word list. With each example, present a way to approach the problem organizationally.

For example:

  In social studies, they would collect the facts and then organize them in the proper fashion.

  For a math problem, they could break down each step and do each one slowly and methodically.

  In spelling, they could make up clues such as a sentence using each letter of the spelling word as a first letter of a word in the sentence. For example, the word *rhyme* could be *Robin Hid Your Money Envelope.*

- Distribute a copy of each student's test scores from Session 1 and the test scores earned since the group began. Have the students compare their test scores earned after they joined the group with those earned prior to being a member of the group. Discuss whether any progress has been made and why or why not.

- Remind the students that this is their final group meeting. Thank them for their cooperation and encourage them to continue using the techniques they have learned in the last six sessions.

(*Note:* The leader may want to meet periodically with the students, individually or in a group setting, to provide ongoing support.)

TEST-TAKING TECHNIQUES
(Grades 4-5)

Tests come in various forms. There are teacher-made tests, standardized tests, oral tests, and pop quizzes. In almost every classroom in every grade, there are students who do their work conscientiously, get good grades on homework and classroom assignments, and fall down when it comes to taking a test on materials both you and they know they understand.

Sometimes this happens because they are nervous at the thought of taking a test and "freeze." Their brains suddenly cannot transfer the knowledge they have to the test questions. Sometimes it is because of a lack of test-taking skills. They know the material, but when faced with many different types of questions about it, they again "freeze."

This group is designed to help students:

- Understand the different methods for answering questions on tests
- Learn how to study for a test

Group candidates:

- Students who do well in classwork but have difficulty with testing situations (*Note:* Students who do not do well with classwork should not be considered for this group. It is impossible to tell how these students are affected by testing situations, because they do not try to do their daily work.)
- Only students who wish to participate should be included in the group
- Six to eight students from the same grade level

Group preparation:

Interview each student selected individually and explain the purpose and process of the group. Then send a parent notification and permission letter (page 215).

Dear _____,

Test-taking is an important part not only of the educational system, but also of life. Throughout life, we will be asked to take tests for one thing or another. Many will be job-related and will determine whether we are hired or promoted to a better position.

Some students do well in their classwork but "freeze up" when it comes to taking a teacher-made or standardized test. One reason for this is that they are not sure of the best way to answer different types of test questions. Your child's classroom teacher has identified your child as one of these students.

In an effort to help your child and others learn more about this issue, I am forming a counseling group that will focus on helping children learn test-taking techniques. They will explore different types of test-taking questions and learn strategies for answering them.

There will be six group meetings scheduled at a time the classroom teacher selects.

Your child knows about the group and has indicated that he or she would like to participate. However, no child is ever included in a small-group counseling program without his or her parents' knowledge and permission.

Please indicate, by completing the form below, that you wish to have your child participate in this group or that you do not want him or her to be included.

Return the permission slip to me by _____.

Thank you,

✂ -

☐ I, _____, *give permission* for my child to partici-
pate in the small-group counseling program to learn test-taking techniques.

☐ I, _____, *do not give permission* for my child to
participate in the small-group counseling program to learn test-taking techniques.

Child's Name _____   Date _____

School _____   Grade _____

Teacher _____

Home Phone (____) _____   Work Phone (____) _____

Parent's Printed Name _____

Parent's Signature _____

215

INTRODUCTION

Objective:

To encourage the students to express their thoughts about tests

Materials Needed:

For each student:
- ☑ Marker

For the leader:
- ☑ 6 large sheets of newsprint
- ☑ Marker
- ☑ Masking tape
- ☑ Paper
- ☑ Pencil

Session Preparation:

Label each piece of newsprint with one of the following phrases:

I think tests are …
Tests make me feel …
One reason we have tests is to …
My teacher thinks tests are …
My friends think tests are …
If there were no tests, I …

Tape the newsprint papers to the wall. Gather any other necessary materials.

Session:

- Introduce the group by telling the students to look at the unfinished sentences on each piece of paper. Then have each student introduce him/herself and tell which piece of newsprint he/she would like to write on first.

- Distribute a marker to each student and instruct the students to begin with the piece of newsprint they said they would like to write on first and write an answer that will finish the sentence. They should sign their names to their work.

- Tell them to continue to write on each piece of newsprint, finishing each sentence and signing their names.

- Have the students look at the completed sentences on each piece of newsprint and discuss their similarities and differences.

- Conclude the session by asking each student to respond aloud to the sentence:

  One thing I would like to learn from these sessions is …

  Record each student's answer on a piece of paper. Save the paper for future reference.

- At the end of the session, take the newsprint papers down. Save them for the final session.

STANDARDIZED TESTS

Objective:

To help students become familiar with standardized tests and the reasons they are given

Materials Needed:

For each student:
☐ None

For the leader:
☑ Sample test booklets of the standardized tests used in the students' school
☑ Chalkboard and chalk or chart paper and marker

Session Preparation:

Collect sample copies of standardized tests the students have already taken. Be sure not to include any tests the students will take in the future. Gather any other necessary materials.

Session:

• Begin the session by asking the students if they know what a standardized test is. (Write *Standardized Test* on the board/chart paper.) Before continuing, make sure the students know that a standardized test is a test purchased from a testing company. It is not a test that the school or teacher makes up. The questions in a standardized test are given to students all over the country and the purpose of the test is to compare students in different parts of the country. It is not a test they are graded on, and it does not appear on their report card. (*Note:* If the students are mature enough, provide information about different standardized tests. Tell the students a standardized test can be an I.Q. test that measures their abilities to learn or an achievement test that measures what they have learned. Discuss the difference between what a student *can learn* and what he/she *has learned.*)

• Explain to the students the standardized testing schedule for their school. Tell them the name of the test, the time of the year it is given, and the grades in which it is given. (At this point, most of the students will realize they have taken a standardized test and will be able to talk about the experience.)

• Discuss how the students feel when taking a standardized test. As the students express their feelings, have them explain the reasons for their feelings.

• Tell the students that people sometimes feel uneasy or nervous when they are not sure of the best way to do something. The first thing they need to know is whether it is better to guess at an answer they do not know or leave it blank. This depends on how the test is scored. Ask the person administering the test how it is scored. If an unanswered question is considered wrong, they might as well take a chance and guess. Standardized tests are usually timed so it is best to answer the questions they know, skip the ones they don't know, then come back, after finishing the test, to the ones they were unable to do the first time.

• Explain that there is more to doing well in a standardized test than answering the questions. It is important to make sure that the answer they are marking is the correct answer for the question they are reading. They must never mark two answers or the question will be wrong. If they must erase, they must erase very clearly so it doesn't look like two answers for the same question. They must remember that these tests are scored by a machine, and the machine will not guess what they meant.

- Conclude the session by reviewing the purpose of these tests. Emphasize that a standardized test is only one measurement of students' ability or achievement, and that although it should be taken seriously, it does not provide a complete picture.

Objective:

To help evaluate the types of questions given on teacher-made tests and learn strategies for answering the questions

Materials Needed:

For each student:
- ☑ Paper
- ☑ Pencil

For the leader:
- ☑ Chalkboard and chalk or chart paper and marker
- ☑ Marker
- ☑ Masking tape

Session Preparation:

Gather the necessary materials.

Session:

- Ask the students to name the kinds of questions asked by teachers on tests. Record their answers on the board/chart paper. (True/false, multiple choice, fill-in-the-blank, matching, essay, etc.)

- Ask the students to prioritize the types of tests from the easiest (1) to the hardest (5). Write each student's name and the priority number after the type of test on the board/chart paper.

- Ask the students to prioritize how upset these tests make them from least upset (1) to most upset (5). Write each student's name and the priority number after the type of test on the board/chart paper.

- Discuss the students' priorities and why they feel each type of test is easy or difficult.

- Tell the students that knowing the following tips can make test-taking easier:

    True/false questions using the words *always* or *never* are usually false.

    In four-choice multiple-choice questions, two choices are usually easy to eliminate, narrowing the choice to two.

    If matching questions have an equal number of words and ideas to be matched, first answer the ones you know.

    When answering essay questions, state the main idea, then write as many things as you can think of about the main idea.

    Fill-in-the-blank questions give no clues. You either know the answer or you don't.

- Distribute paper and a pencil to each student. Tell the students to think about what was just said about true/false questions and make up three questions apiece. Then have each student present his/her questions to the group.

- Remind the students what was said about essay questions. Give the group a question which they can easily answer. (Who is the President of the United States and what does the President do?) Have the group answer it together while you record the answer on the board/chart paper.

- Conclude the session by having each student complete this sentence:

    I really thought the most difficult kind of test question was _____. Now I think the most difficult kind of test question is _____.

OBSERVING TEST-TAKING IN SELF AND OTHERS

Objective:

To allow students to observe their own reactions and those of other students in a test-taking situation

Materials Needed:

For each student:
☑ Pencil
☑ Copy of *Test-Taking Test* (page 221)

For the leader:
☐ None

Session Preparation:

Reproduce *Test-Taking Test* for each student. Gather any other necessary materials.

Session:

• Distribute the *Test-Taking Test* and a pencil to each student. Place the test paper face down and tell the students not to turn it over until you say they may do so.

• Tell the students to turn their papers over and begin. (*Note:* The test is a series of meaningless questions. If the students do not read the first direction which says, "Read this entire test before beginning work," they will perform unnecessary tasks. When they reach the last question, their mistake will become clear. As the students begin to catch onto the "trick," they will begin to observe other students who are still working.)

• Discuss the activity by asking the following questions:

When did you realize you were not to do anything but the last question?

How did you feel when you found out you had been "tricked"?

What did you notice about the behavior of the other students?

Do you think other students would react the same way you did?

• Conclude the session by asking the students to tell on a scale of 1 (least) to 10 (greatest) how important it is to carefully read the directions before starting a test.

Name_____   Date_____

TEST-TAKING TEST

Directions: Read this test through completely before beginning work.

1. Who is the President of the United States? _____

2. What is the color of most apples?_____

3. What does the + sign stand for in a math problem? _____

4. How many children are in this group? _____

5. Name a famous person. _____

6. Write the vowels in the alphabet. _____

7. Where would you go to check out a book you would like to read? _____

8. Name a large bird. _____

9. Circle the best answer. This test was: **EASY   SO SO   HARD**

10. Write the date of your birthday, but do not answer questions 1 through 9. _____

GROUPS TO GO: SMALL GROUPS FOR COUNSELORS ON THE GO © 2006 MAR✴CO PRODUCTS, INC. 1-800-448-2197

Session 5
HOW TO STUDY FOR A TEST

Objective:

To help students learn how to study for a test

Materials Needed:

For each student:
- ☑ Pencil
- ☑ Paper
- ☑ Article appropriate for the grade level of the students

For the leader:
- ☐ None

Session Preparation:

Reproduce a copy of the article for each student. Gather any other necessary materials.

Session:

- Begin the session by asking the students to name some good ways to study for a test. Encourage the students to talk about the ways they study, the amount of time it takes to study for a test, and whether what they are doing is working.

- If "making up a test" is mentioned as one good way to study for a test, tell the students they are going to further explore one of the ways mentioned. If this was not mentioned, tell the students they are going to try a new way to study for a test. Tell them that one of the best ways to study for a test is to make one up at home.

- Distribute a copy of the article, a pencil, and paper to each student. Have the students put their names on their paper. Tell them to first read the article completely, then go back through it and make up test questions about it. In order to cover every possible type of question, they should have some true/false, multiple-choice, fill-in-the blank, matching, and one essay question. Explain that they must work alone and tell them how much time they have to complete the task.

- When the allotted time has elapsed, collect the tests. Shuffle the tests and pass them out to a group member other than the one who made up the test. Tell the students how much time they have to answer the questions.

- When the allotted time has elapsed, the test papers should be returned to their originators, who will correct the test.

- After the tests are corrected, conclude the session by asking each student:

  How did you feel when taking the test?

  Did making up the test help you when it came time to take the test?

  Do you think this would be a good way to study for a test?

CONCLUSION AND EVALUATION

Objective:

To identify any changes that have taken place during the group sessions

Materials Needed:

For each student:
- ☑ Marker

For the leader:
- ☑ 6 large sheets of newsprint
- ☑ Marker
- ☑ Masking tape
- ☑ Paper with students' responses to "One thing I would like to learn from this group is..." from Session 1
- ☑ Paper
- ☑ Pencil
- ☑ 6 newsprint sheets from Session 1

Session Preparation:

Label each piece of newsprint with one of the following titles:

> I think tests are …
> Tests make me feel …
> One reason we have tests is to …
> My teacher thinks tests are …
> My friends think tests are …
> If there were no tests, I …

Tape each piece of newsprint to the wall, far enough apart to fit the newsprint sheet with same sentence from Session 1 next to each sheet. Gather any other necessary materials.

Session:

- Distribute markers to the students and tell them to write their answers to the sentences and sign their name on the pieces of newsprint.

- When the students have finished, bring out the newsprint sheets from Session 1. Tape them beside the newsprint sheets for this session that have the same titles.

- Tell the students to look at both sessions' sentences and discuss any changes that seem to have taken place as well as those that have remained the same.

- Ask the students to respond aloud to the sentence, "One thing I learned from this group was..." Record the answers on a piece of paper, then compare these responses with the responses given in Session 1.

- Conclude the group by thanking the students for their cooperation and wishing them luck on their future test-taking adventures.

223

ABOUT THE AUTHOR

Arden Martenz is the president of Mar∗co Products. She is the author/coauthor of more that 30 books relating to the field of guidance. She was an elementary teacher in grades three and five, an elementary counselor for 19 years, and a graduate instructor for classroom management in Pennsylvania.

A graduate of the University of Washington in Seattle, Washington and a holder of a Master's Degree in guidance and counseling from Lehigh University in Pennsylvania, she now spends her time creating materials for guidance counselors and presenting workshops throughout the country. In the year 2000, she was named an outstanding educator in Bucks County for the previous century.

She is married, has two sons and a daughter, and six grandchildren.